Quilted Bags & Totes

Denise Clason

©2006 Denise Clason
Published by

krause publications
An Imprint of F+W Publications

700 East State Street • Iola, WI 54990-0001
715-445-2214 • 888-457-2873

Our toll-free number to place an order or obtain a free catalog is (800) 258-0929.

The following registered trademark terms, products and companies appear in this publication:
Singer®, Baby Lock®, Bernina® of America, Brother®, Elna USA, Fairfield Processing Corp., White®, Quilter's Star, Kenmore®, Pfaff, Janome, Gingher, Collins®, Tacony Corp., Husqvarna® Viking® Sewing Machine Co., June Tailor™ Quilt Basting Spray, Sew Station™, Olfa®, Prym® Consumer USA, InnerFuse™, Fray Check™, EZ Quilting®, Rowenta, The Warm™ Co., Steam-a-Seam2®, Warm & Natural, C&T Publishing, fast2fuse®, Timtex™, Mettler, Gutermann, Coats & Clark®, Pellon®, Wonder Under®, P&B Textiles, RJR Fabrics, Sulky®, KK2000™ Temporary Spray Adhesive, Blendables® Thread, Fairfield, Mountain Mist® Cream Rose® batting, Clover, Atlas Nitrile Touch™ Quilter's Gloves, Schmetz Needles, Lickity Grip®, Velcro®, Omnigrip®, Omnigrid®, Offray®, JHB Stitchin' Up the Pieces Buttons, Beacon Adhesives, Gem-Tac®, Fabri-Tac®, DMC®, The Beadery®, 3-n-1 tool, Salway beads, Beadalon®, C-Thru® ¼" ruler, Clover, General's®, Strapworks, Expo International, Fiskars®, Antique Textiles, Nifty-Thrifty Dry Goods, Ancient Earth Echoes Designs, Wrights®, Coats, Blumenthal Lansing.

Library of Congress Catalog Number: 2006922399

ISBN 13: 978-0-89689-386-3
ISBN 10: 0-89689-386-3

Designed by Dana Boll of BookBuster Publishing Services and Marilyn McGrane
Edited by Susan Sliwicki

Printed in The United States of America

ACKNOWLEDGMENTS

I WANT TO THANK Krause Publications for the wonderful opportunity that I've had working on "Quilted Bags & Totes." Writing my first book with Krause, "New Country Quilting," was one of the highlights in my career; working with Krause on another book became the next highlight.

The staff at Krause has been wonderful, especially Candy Wiza, Krause's new book acquisition editor. We have become friends in the last few years while we worked on my first book and began to get this book "in the works." A big thank-you goes to Susan Sliwicki, my editor, for trusting in my creativity and giving me room to grow in the process. You both have been great examples of what it takes to put a good book together.

I also need to mention the book team's designer, Marilyn McGrane. When I saw the layout on my first book, I was just ecstatic! The design and layout of the book surpassed any dreams that I had! Thank you for your creativity in the book design and making it a book that people open just to look at it, because it is so beautiful.

A big thank-you goes out to my family. Pat, my husband, is constantly giving me a thumbs up on my design work, telling me, "You can do that!" With his support, I have.

My family has been a big part of why I do what I do. I love to be around them, and working from home has given me that wonderful opportunity. Thank you also to my daughter, Erin, and my son, Matthew, who always encourage me and allow me to do what I love to do — sew and quilt!

Last but not least, thank you to all of you fellow purse lovers. This book is for you! Please enjoy these designs and create many beautiful masterpieces.

TABLE OF CONTENTS

INTRODUCTION

THERE IS — AND ALWAYS HAS BEEN — A FASCINATION BETWEEN WOMEN AND THEIR PURSES.

WE GIRLS LOVE anything that we can use to hold our "girly" things. We can't go anywhere unless we have the right bag or tote with us. We treasure and protect our purses; some of us — namely my grandmother — like to keep our purses in our laps during dinners out in restaurants! We get attached to our purses, and we have our favorites — a lot of favorites. We love looking at them, buying them and admiring — OK, maybe coveting — the ones our friends have.

I've loved purses and bags ever since I was a little girl and first was introduced to them by my mother, as I'm sure her mother introduced them to her. My daughter, who now is 21, is the only person with whom I go purse shopping. We both love to spend time looking at each purse, making sure we know everything that it does, and, more importantly, how much it will hold.

Each purse needs to have its own individual purpose in order for me to feel it is worth buying. If I want a purse to be functional, it has to be functional. When I'm looking for a dressy purse, I want it to be dressy. Sometimes, I just fall in love with a purse and simply have to have it.

We all need to have enough purses, bags or totes to fit into the many needs of our lives. That is why I have designed different types of purses, bags and totes for this book. Some are for work, while others are dressy, casual or sporty. A few are here because I just wanted to make them!

I've been making purses, bags and totes for myself, my friends and my family for as long as I can remember. I loved designing the purses, bags and totes in this book; I hope you have fun as you create them. Feel free to find your own combinations of colors. Play at the fabric store, and pick colors that feel right with each other. Envision how each bag will look once it is completed, and make sure you still think it is right. You may find that you need to change fabrics or embellishments to make your bag look perfect. Just trust your creativity and enjoy!

CHAPTER 1

Getting Started

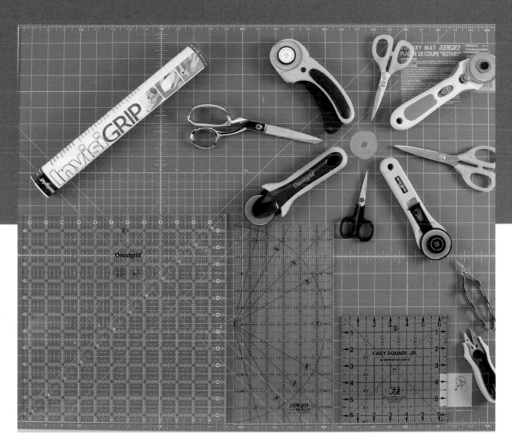

THE RIGHT TOOLS, supplies and techniques will make your sewing and quilting more enjoyable. Refer to the Contributors and Resources section in the back of the book for more information about the products featured in this book.

Tools and Supplies

Get each project off to a great start by planning ahead. Stock your sewing area with these basic tools and supplies.

Cutting Tools

You'll use a rotary cutter for most fabric cutting. There are many varieties of rotary cutters available, and they come in several different sizes and styles. I like the Olfa rotary cutter I first purchased when I began quilting about 18 years ago. Select the variety of cutters that work best for you.

Cutting mats and rotary cutters go hand in hand. A good cutting mat is a lifesaver for you, your table and your rotary cutting blades. I like having several sizes of mats on hand. I keep a 12" x 18" mat right next to my sewing machine to cut the little pieces off of my blocks or small pieces that I need for a project. I keep a larger 24" x 36" mat on my counter for cutting most of my project pieces. Find the mats that fit your work style and space. Just be sure to protect your mats from direct sunlight and heat, which will warp them. Keep those glue guns away, too.

There are many different rulers from which to choose. Rotary rulers make your sewing and quilting so much easier. They will be your best friends as you quilt.

You will want the following basic rulers to complete the projects in this book: 12" square, 6" square, 6" x 24" and 6" x 12". The more you quilt, the more specialized rulers you may want.

You'll also want good-quality fabric and thread scissors; I like Gingher scissors. Using fabric and thread scissors will help your cuts to be more accurate.

Keep your scissors nice and sharp by marking them with a ribbon or label that says "fabric." Let's hope that others in your household take the hint!

Sewing Machine

Whether you're working with an older machine or breaking in a brand-new model, you'll want to keep your sewing machine in top form to get the best possible performance. Keep up with maintenance as directed in your manual, and master the basics, such as oiling the machine and changing needles.

Save time and frustration by keeping the basics on hand, such as spare bobbins, machine oil and fresh needles. Be sure to change needles with each new project to get the best results.

Presser Feet

Several presser feet are useful for creating these projects. Each project includes a list of materials, supplies and tools, including the specialty presser feet that will be used.

Most sewing machines come with a walking foot. If yours didn't, I recommend that you buy one. I love this tool! The walking foot comes in very handy when you are quilting straight lines, stitching in the ditch and sewing on bindings. It keeps the binding and the quilted project moving through the machine together, which prevents the top of the quilt from twisting as you sew. I also use this foot to stitch in the ditch after the binding is sewn on.

A ¼" foot, also called a quilting foot, will come in handy for many of these projects and other quilting projects that you will make. Use this foot to sew accurate ¼" seams.

The darning foot is great for free-motion machine quilting. The opening at the base of the foot lets you see exactly where you are quilting and what you have quilted — two very important things! I lower my feed dogs while using the darning foot to allow for more movement and freedom. If you're trying free-motion quilting for the first time, practice first on some extra fabric and batting. You'll find your comfort zone in no time, and then you'll be ready to move on to your project.

Pressing Tools

Pressing is important in sewing and quilting. It really makes the item look professional. You'll also want an iron and ironing board when you're working with fusibles.

Find the tools that work best for you, and check out your workstation to make sure those tools are easily accessible. Some pressing boards are made to go on the table top, so they don't take up much room. Those are very nice to have. Some ironing boards can be set at table height, so all you have to do is turn your chair, and you're ready to press.

I keep my ironing board right next to my sewing machine so that it's close to my work space. You will be getting up and down a lot. I do have to admit that it is nice to get up and down every once in a while.

Notions and General Tools

You'll use a variety of notions to make the projects in this book. Here are some of my tried-and-true favorites.

Pins: Good-quality pins are always worth the price. I prefer the glass-head silk pins, because they are easy to see and handle. These pins also pierce fabrics well, even when you are going through three layers of fabric and batting.

Pincushion: A pincushion is a vital sewing room accessory. Whether you like the convenience of a wrist-style cushion, the security of a magnetic one or the whimsy of a collectible pincushion, there are plenty of choices to help you keep track of your pins.

Needles: You'll need both machine and hand sewing needles to complete these projects. There are machine quilting needles made specifically for your sewing machine; pick some up at your favorite quilt shop. Machine quilting needles work the best because they are made for repetitive motion and keep the thread from breaking at the fast speeds you'll achieve while you are free-motion quilting. My favorite machine quilting needles are the size 80/12 needles made by Schmetz.

Marking Tools: The right marking tools will make your work easier. For appliqué work, you'll want a fine-point permanent marker. A white chalk pencil comes in handy for general sewing; I prefer General's white chalk pencil.

Eyelets and Eyelet Tools: Several projects, including the Yorkshire bag, call for eyelets. In addition to the eyelets, you'll need the tool to apply them. I prefer the line of eyelets and tools available through Prym Consumer USA.

Beads and Beading Tools: You can add a lot of flair to a bag by creating a beaded zipper pull. If you enjoy beading, you probably have the tools and supplies to create this simple embellishment. If you don't, you'll want a few basic tools and supplies. I like The Beadery's 3-in-1 Tool, which combines a wire cutter, straight pliers and round nose pliers so you can curl, cut and bend wire. You'll also need beads to suit your project, and eye pins to create the pull; I like the gilded eye pins from Beadalon.

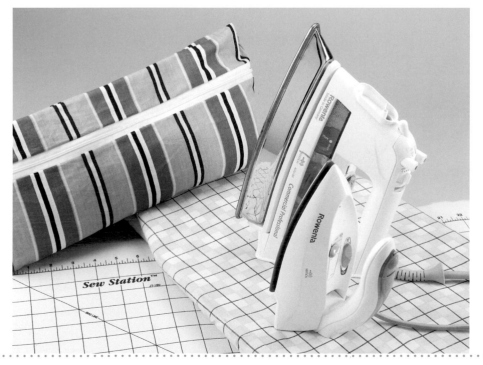

Lickity Grip: This new product is wonderful for craft work where your hands need help gripping. Lickity Grip is great for machine quilting; it helps your fingertips grip the project, which reduces hand and arm fatigue.

Anti-Fray Solution: Keep ribbons and trim looking picture perfect by using this product to prevent fraying. I prefer Fray Check by Prym Consumer USA; it dries clear and is machine washable.

Basting Products: When it comes to basting, you can use thread, pins or spray adhesives; there are a variety of products on the market to fit your needs. Find the method that works the best for you.

I prefer using Sulky KK2000 Temporary Spray Adhesive; it really speeds up basting.

Thread: Select threads that match your fabrics, and keep staples such as black, white, tan (used for most piecing) and invisible on hand, too. I like the all-purpose threads available from Coats.

Adhesives: Several projects call for craft glues. I like Fabri-Tac and Gem-Tac by Beacon Adhesives. Fabri-Tac works great for a variety of uses, including leather, silk flowers, trims and ribbons, while Gem-Tac craft glue is ideal for working with metal findings and rhinestones.

Stiletto tool: A stiletto tool makes

it so much easier — and safer — to work with fabric in tight spaces. Use it to adjust fabric when you're stitching straight or curved seams, pressing appliques or positioning or sewing trims or embellishments.

Seam ripper: I almost hate to mention this tool, because we are all so proficient! But, occasionally you will need a seam ripper; I admit that I did have some experiences with one during the process of this book. Find a seam ripper that fits comfortably and works well for you.

Fabrics

Choosing fabrics is one of my favorite things to do! I love putting combinations together.

The best and most enjoyable way to select fabrics is to dig in and surround yourself with colors and patterns.

Don't be shy; take the bolts from the shelves and unroll them and lay them on top of other fabrics. Look at the patterns, and see how the colors blend with each other. Notice how the fabrics drape and wrinkle. Squish the fabric in your hand and release it to see if there are wrinkles; if it is a nice quality cotton, it won't wrinkle as much.

Choose colors that you like and that go well together. Don't choose very light pastel colors to go with very dark colors; make sure they blend and coordinate. Look at the photos in this book for suggestions on fabric combinations. Most importantly, have fun.

Unless otherwise specified, use 100 percent cotton fabric to make the projects in this book. Prewash all of your fabric pieces in cold water, and dry them on a cool setting. If you are using small scraps, place them in a nylon stocking that is tied at the end so you won't lose them in the wash. Press the pieces to get them ready for cutting.

Batting and Interfacing

Batting, fusible web and interfacing help to add detail, dimension and structure to bags and totes.

I recommend that you use a 100 percent cotton batting for the best results in these projects. I prefer Mountain Mist Cream Rose batting, and I also like Wonder Under fusible web by Pellon. Find the products that work the best for you.

Stiff, fusible interfacings used to create fabric boxes, bowls and vases are great for bags, too. These products include InnerFuse by Prym Consumer USA, fast2fuse by C&T Publishing and Timtex by Timber Lane Press. These products are ideal for creating inserts for the bottoms of bags and totes to give them extra support and strength.

Handles and Straps

While most of the projects in this book use fabric handles or straps you'll sew yourself, you can choose to customize your bags and totes with specialty handles or straps.

Webbing is perfect to make strong, adjustable straps, such as those featured on the Messenger and Bradford bags. Webbing comes in a variety of colors and widths.

String beads on wire to make an elegant handle. Search the home décor section of your favorite fabric shop to find drapery cording that makes a fun and elegant handle, such as in the Danielle Bag. If the hardware store is more your style, find inspiration in dowels or metal chain link, such as that used to create the strap for the April Bag. Or, finish the project faster by using ready-made leather, wood, metal chain or plastic handles.

Webbing, Closures and Hardware

Add a practical, professional-looking touch to your bags and totes with the right webbing, closures and hardware. D-rings, slide rings and swivel hooks go hand in hand with webbing. Eyelets are another way to add handles or straps to a bag, while zippers, elastic, buckles, magnetic closures and hook-and-loop tape are great ways to keep pockets and purses closed. All of these products come in various sizes and styles to fit your projects. Find what works best for you.

Embellishments

Add a custom touch to your bags with embellishments. From buttons and beads to ribbons and rickrack, you're sure to find something you like. Embellishments used in this book include embroidery floss, buttons, beads, ribbon, custom trims, fiber trims, tassels, piping and cording.

Techniques

• • • • •
Adding Appliqué

Appliqué adds a great touch to projects, such as the hearts featured on the Cottage Tote. Here's how to do it:

1 Place fusible web over the appliqué pattern. Use a permanent pen to trace the pattern onto the smooth paper side of the fusible web.

2 Cut around the pen line, leaving about ¼" excess.

3 Iron the fusible web onto the wrong side of the fabric.

4 Once the fused fabric has cooled, cut out the shape on the pen line. Peel the paper backing off of the appliqué shape.

5 Iron the appliqué to the right side of the fabric as indicated. Place a piece of paper or tear-away stabilizer underneath the appliqué shape.

6 With matching thread in the needle and the bobbin, finish the edges of the appliqué with a small zigzag satin stitch. Or, you can blanket stitch around the edges by hand or machine.

7 Secure the edges of the appliqué with anti-fray solution.

• • • • •
Making the Blanket Stitch

The blanket stitch is useful for finishing appliqué shapes, such as the hearts on the front of the Cottage Tote.

1 Bring the needle up at A, and pull the thread through. Hold the thread beneath the needle to form a loop.

2 Insert the needle into the fabric at B, and bring it back to the surface at C. Pull the needle through, adjusting the tension of the loop as you go, so you have a flat stitch without any puckers. The blanket stitch loops should be evenly spaced. I space mine about ¼" apart and about ¼" in stitch length.

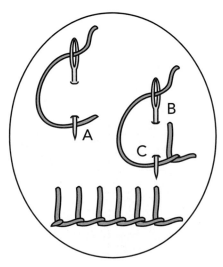

Blanket Stitch

Basting

Traditional hand basting and the new, timesaving temporary spray adhesives both work well for basting. I was enlightened this year when I found out how convenient quilt basting spray is. I love it!

Basting With Temporary Spray Adhesive

1 Lay an old sheet over the ironing board to protect it. Iron the backing piece face down. If it isn't too big, you can leave it on the ironing board, and lay the batting piece on top of the backing.

2 Spray the basting spray over the batting; avoid getting the spray on the ironing board.

3 Lay the finished top or fabric face up over the batting; use your hands to smooth it out. Pinning the edges is fine. This method works very well as long as you cover the batting's surface with basting spray.

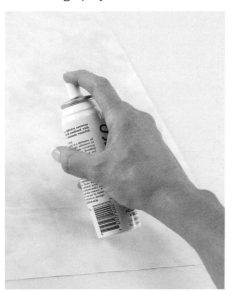

Hand Basting

1 Layer the backing (face down), batting and finished top (face up).

2 With a sharp hand sewing needle and contrasting thread (dark thread for light fabric colors and light thread for dark fabric colors), make large running stitches going in two different directions as shown. There is no need to put a knot in the thread, as you will pull these threads out after you have completed the machine or hand quilting.

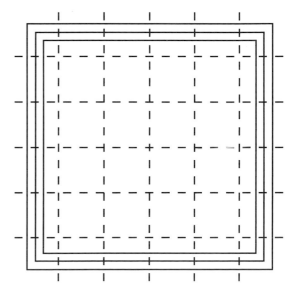

Basting Pattern

Creating Bias Strips

1 Locate the true bias by folding the fabric so the crosswise edge is parallel to the lengthwise grain (selvage).

2 Press the fabric along the diagonal fold; use the crease as a guide.

3 Position a cutting ruler along the creased line. Space your rotary cuts by the width desired.

4 Piece the strips, right sides together, as needed to make one continuous bias-binding strip.

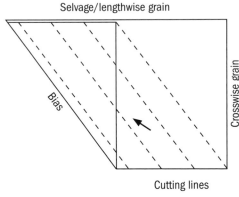

Selvage/lengthwise grain

Bias

Crosswise grain

Cutting lines

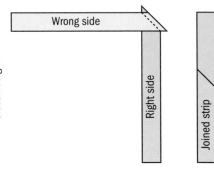

Wrong side

Right side

Joined strip

Making Handles

Each fabric purse or tote handle will be a different size, but the sewing is all the same. Here are basic instructions to complete fabric handles for the bags in this book.

1 Press ¼" on one side of the lengthwise handle strip to the wrong side of the strip.

2 Position a strip of batting down the center of the strip.

3 Fold the unhemmed side of the strip just over the center of the batting.

4 Fold the ¼" hemmed side of the strip over the raw edge. Pin the strip in place.

5 Topstitch along the edge of the center fold and on either side of the center stitching.

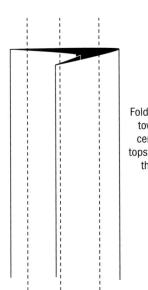

Fold the strips toward the center, and topstitch along the edge.

Making Purse Corners

Purse corners may seem tricky, but this no-fail method makes it easy.

1 With right sides together, fold the tote so that the side seam meets up with the bottom tote or purse seam. You will need to peek inside of the purse to make sure that the seams line up.

2 Pin the seams together so that they stay in place.

3 Sew across the corner of the tote according to the measurement given in the pattern.

4 Zigzag stitch next to the seam.

5 Cut off any extra fabric.

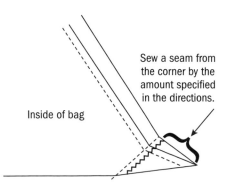

Inside of bag

Sew a seam from the corner by the amount specified in the directions.

Making Bag Base Inserts

Add strength and stability to your totes and bags with a removable insert made of stiff, fusible interfacing that is covered with fabric.

1 Cut the stiff, fusible interfacing and two rectangles of fabric to the size directed; in general, the interfacing and fabric will be slightly smaller than the measurements for the bottom of the bag to allow enough room for the interfacing to be covered in fabric and still be removed easily.

2 Cover the stiff, fusible interfacing with two rectangles of fabric, right side out. Iron the fabric onto each side of the fusible interfacing to cover it completely.

3 Zigzag stitch around all four edges of the fabric-covered insert.

4 Place the insert in the bottom of the purse.

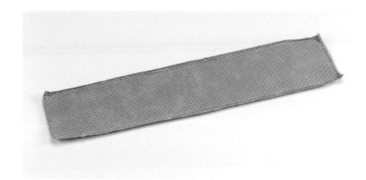

Quilting

Machine Quilting

Machine quilting has become very popular, as it provides numerous design options. All of the projects in this book were machine quilted; you can see the pattern used if you look closely at the photos. It is up to you what type of quilting design you choose. Just be sure to practice!

1 If needed, change the presser foot on your sewing machine. I use a darning foot for stippling, but a walking foot may come in handy on patterns where straight stitching is recommended.

2 When using a darning foot, lower the feed dogs so it is easier to maneuver the project.

3 Position your hands on the project, one on either side of the needle. To make a stippling effect, move the project in the direction you desire. Avoid spinning the project; the design will flow if you keep the piece in the same direction.

4 When you reach the edge of the project, turn it at the corners, then begin stippling in the next direction.

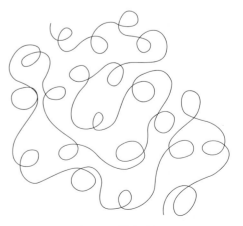

Loopy quilt design

Hand Quilting

A few basic supplies make it easy to hand quilt your pieces. Look for a good-quality thread that has quilting thread written on the label. I use a size 12 betweens needle, which is a very small, thin needle that pierces the fabric better and is easier to move up and down through the fabric. Find a thimble that works best for you, too. I prefer thimbles that have a ridge on the edge to keep the needle from slipping off. Give hand quilting a try; you may find that it is something you can't live without!

1 Plan the desired quilting pattern. You may wish to use a chalk pencil to mark the pattern on the project.

2 Knot the thread, and bury the knot in the batting layer so the knot is hidden.

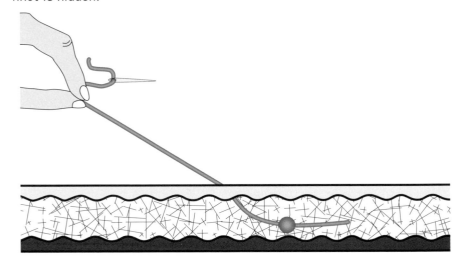

3 Stitch through all three layers loading several stitches on the needle at once.

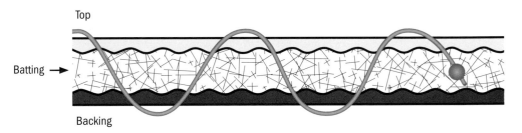

4 When you're out of thread, knot the thread twice to end off. Bury the knots in the batting.

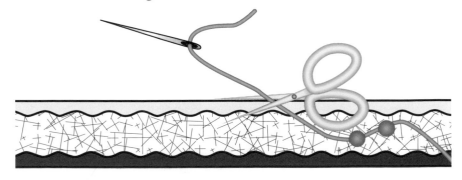

Binding the Bags

The bindings in this book all are made from 2¼"-wide bias strips. I've found that I can get a "clean" look with this size of bias strip vs. the 2½"-wide strips that sometimes are recommended. I use a walking foot when applying binding, when it is appropriate. Sometimes the space is not big enough to fit the walking foot in the purse projects, so your ¼" foot will work just fine.

1 Measure the distance around the purse or tote bag. Cut and sew enough bias strips to go around the measured distance.

2 Press the bias strip seams open, then press the strip in half lengthwise, wrong sides together.

3 Pin the ironed bias strip, raw edges together, to the middle or center of the edge needing binding. Sew the bias strip onto the bag. Stop ¼" from the edge of the bag, backstitch three or four stitches. If the binding is applied too loosely, the edges will ruffle up. if the binding is pulled with too much tension, the edges will curl up. If the edges lie flat, a slight hint of tension or no tension is all that's needed. Adjust the tension as needed.

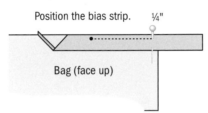

Position the bias strip.　¼"

Stop ¼" from the end of the quilt, and backstitch three or four stitches.

4 When you get to the corner, flip the binding straight up.

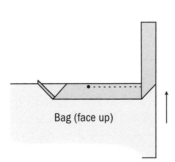

5 Fold the binding back down at a 90-degree angle. Sew three or four backstitches. Continue sewing the binding on with the perfect amount of tension. Repeat Steps 4 and 5 for each remaining corner and side.

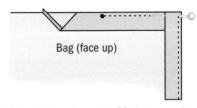

Fold the binding down at a 90-degree angle.

6 When you get to the end of the binding, tuck the tail end of the binding underneath the first binding layer, and topstitch both layers to secure them.

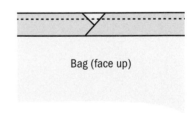

7 After the binding is sewn, turn the folded edge to the back or to the inside of the project. Pin the folded edge over the seam line, approximately 2" apart. Stitch in the ditch from the top of the project to hold the binding in place. Use invisible thread or a thread that matches the background fabric color. If desired, hand sew the binding to the inside of the bag.

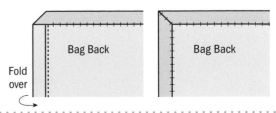

Fold over

Stitching in the Ditch/ Topstitching

Stitching in the ditch, or topstitching, is excellent for quilting when you don't want to feature a distinct quilting pattern, especially when there are a lot of pieces involved in the block or quilt.

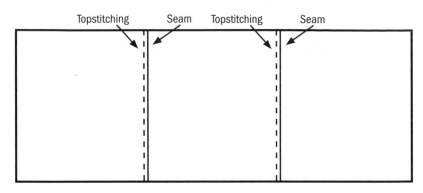

Topstitching Seam Topstitching Seam

1 Position the needle so the topstitch falls just a fraction away from the actual seam, on the side opposite of the pressed seam. Keeping the stitches away from the actual seam makes the quilting stronger and makes it less likely to break the seam.

Adding Zippers

Here are some basic tips for installing zippers. Some zippers don't come in the exact lengths and colors required for the projects, but that's OK. In that case, zigzag stitch over the area just ¼" short of the end of the piece, and trim the zipper off.

Sew ¼" from the edge of the fabric and zipper.

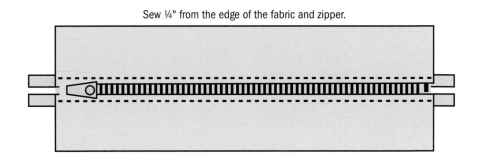

1 Position the metal tip of the zipper ¼" from the end of the project, right sides together, to the top raw edge of the fabric or project.

2 Pin and sew ¼" from the edge of the fabric and zipper. Backstitch at both ends. Stitch the remaining side of the zipper to the opposite side of the project in the same manner.

3 Zigzag the raw edges.

4 Press the seam allowances toward the fabric.

5 Topstitch close to the edge of the fabric, next to the zipper.

CHAPTER 2

Casual Totes

AMBER'S Tote

WHEN I SAW the floral print that I used in this tote, I had to buy it. I knew exactly what I was going to make as soon as I brought it home. The coordinating green fabric is actually from a set of napkins that I bought for a project one day, and this was it. The fabrics went together perfectly. The ribbon was the ideal touch to finish off the tote. Although it is bright, it gives a wonderful contrast to the whole look. Finished size: 13½" x 16".

YOU WILL NEED

FABRIC

- ½ yd. decorator bright floral, 54" wide (tote)
- ½ yd. coordinating green, 45" wide (tote)
- ½ yd. muslin, 45" wide (backing for quilting)
- ½ yd. decorator yellow and white check, 54" wide (lining, lining pocket, insert)

NOTIONS

- ¾ yd. 100 percent cotton batting
- 1 spool multicolored grosgrain ribbon, ⅞" wide
- ¼ yd. woven, iron-on interfacing (pocket stabilizer)
- All-purpose threads to match fabrics
- Invisible and machine-quilting threads
- Anti-fray solution
- Quilt basting spray
- ¼ yd. stiff, fusible interfacing

TOOLS

- Basic sewing supplies
- Rotary cutting tools
- Presser feet: ¼" foot, darning foot

Instructions
Please read all of the instructions before beginning this project. Refer to Chapter 1: Getting Started for detailed information on tools and techniques. All seams are ¼" wide; use a ¼" foot for accurate seams.

Cut the Materials

FROM	CUT	FOR
Floral print	2 rectangles, 9½" x 17"	Tote
Green print	2 rectangles, 8½" x 17"	Tote
	2 strips, 2¾" x 26"	Handles
Yellow checkerboard	2 rectangles, 16" x 16¾"	Lining
	1 rectangle, 10½" x 16½"	Lining pocket
	2 rectangles, 5¼" x 10½"	Insert
Stiff, fusible interfacing	1 rectangle, 5¼" x 10½"	Insert
Batting	1 strip, 1" x 26"	Handle
Iron-on interfacing	2 rectangles, 10½" x 16½"	Lining pocket

Make the Bag

1 Sew the 8½" x 17" green rectangle to the 9½" x 17" floral decorator rectangle, right sides together, along the 17" side. Press the seam open. Repeat for the remaining two pieces as shown.

2 Cut two pieces of batting and muslin backing 1" larger than the tote front and back.

3 Layer the batting on the muslin backing. Spray the batting with the quilt basting spray, and layer the tote front on top, face up.

4 Using a darning foot and invisible thread, quilt a loopy design over the floral print. See Getting Started for detailed instructions. Use multicolored machine thread to create a beautiful effect on the lower half of the tote (the green area).

5 Cut off the extra batting and backing, then straighten up all of the sides.

6 With right sides together, sew the front and back pieces together along one vertical side. Press the seam open.

7 On the right side of the tote, use invisible thread to closely topstitch on both sides of the vertical seam.

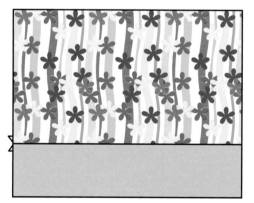

Make two.

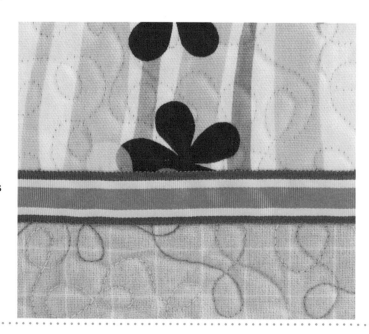

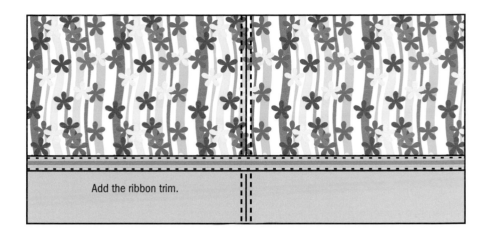

Add the Ribbon Trim

1 Center the multicolored ribbon over the green and floral seam on the tote, and sew it over the seam.

2 Sew along both sides of the ribbon as shown.

Add the ribbon trim.

Sew the Tote Together

1 With right sides together, sew the other side of the tote together. Press the seam open, and topstitch the same as in Make the Bag: Step 7.

2 Sew the tote bottom edge, right sides together. Backstitch at each end. Keep the tote inside out.

3 With right sides together, make a purse corner by sewing across the seams 2½" from the tip of the corner. See Getting Started for details.

Make the Lining

1 With right sides together, sew the two 16" x 16¾" yellow checkerboard decorator pieces along one of the 16¾" sides. Press open. Set aside.

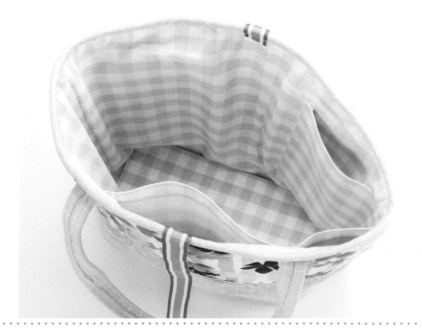

Make the Lining Pocket

1 Press the 10½" x 16½" piece of iron-on interfacing to the wrong side of the 10½" x 16½" pocket lining.

2 Along the 16½" side of the interfaced fabric, fold the edge over by ¼" and press. Fold the edge over by another ¼" and press again.

3 Topstitch along the edge, and then topstitch again ¼" from the line of stitching as shown.

4 Fold the side and bottom edges in ¼", and press the edges to create the hem to prepare for sewing the tote lining.

5 On the right side of the lining fabric, pin the left edge of the pocket so it is 4½" from the sewn seam and 2¼" from the top edge. Sew the pocket along the three sides.

6 Sew two vertical lines of stitching, one along the seam of the lining and the other 3½" from the lining seam as shown.

7 Sew the lining, right sides together, along the side and bottom edges.

8 With right sides together, fold the lining so that the side seam meets up with the bottom seam of the lining. You will need to peek inside the lining to make sure that the seams line up. Pin them together so that they stay in place. Sew 2½" from the corner tip. See Getting Started for details.

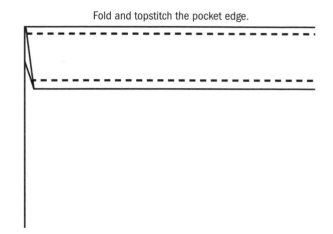

Fold and topstitch the pocket edge.

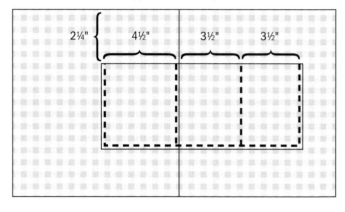

Position, pin and sew the pockets.

2¼" 4½" 3½" 3½"

Sew the Lining Inside the Tote

1 With the wrong side out on the lining, position the lining inside the tote. Pin the top raw edges together.

2 Sew the two fabric pieces together around the top edge of the tote.

Add the Binding

1 Cut 2¼"-wide bias binding from the green fabric to go around the top edge of the tote. See Getting Started for details.

2 Add the binding. See Getting Started for details.

Make the Handles and Ribbon Ties

1 Press a ¼" hem along one 26" edge of each of the 2¾" x 26" handle pieces.

2 Lay a 1" batting strip inside the center of each handle piece. Fold the raw edge of the handle over the batting. Fold the hem side over the raw edge. Pin in place.

3 Stitch down the folded edge of the handle; this topstitch should be down the "center" of the handle. Topstitch along both edges of the handle. See Getting Started for details.

4 Position and sew the handles, right sides together, to the tote so each handle is 1⅝" from the top edge and 4½" from the side seams. Fold the handle up, and topstitch the handle ¼" from the seam as shown.

5 Cut two segments of multicolored ribbon, each 15½" long. Cut one end of each ribbon at an angle. Apply anti-fray solution to both ends of the ribbons, and allow the solution to dry.

6 Sew the straight edge of each ribbon to the inside of the center top of the purse opening; stitch in the ditch or close to the binding.

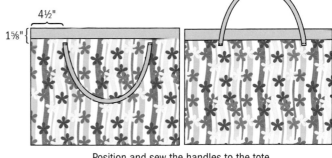

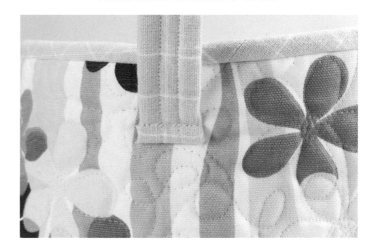

Position and sew the handles to the tote.

Make the Tote Bottom Insert

1 Cover the 5¼" x 10½" piece of stiff, fusible interfacing with two yellow check 5¼" x 10½" rectangles.

2 Iron the fabric onto each side of the fusible interfacing.

3 Zigzag around all four edges of the fabric-covered insert.

4 Place the insert in the bottom of the purse.

KELLIE'S Tote

AMISH QUILTS ARE so beautiful. I always have been drawn to the simplicity of their design and the way they put the colors together. This is my version of an Amish block, using prints in the same great colors that are typically done in solids. For this project, buy prints that read as solids. I embellished the tote with my Stitchin' Up the Pieces Buttons (No. 28270), which are available through JHB. Get inspired from other colors, and make several totes with different color combinations. Finished size: 10¼" x 10½".

YOU WILL NEED

FABRIC

- [ ] 1 fat quarter beige print
- [ ] 1 fat quarter medium purple print
- [ ] 1 fat quarter black print
- [ ] 2 fat quarters medium blue print

NOTIONS

- [ ] ⅓ yd. 100 percent cotton batting
- [ ] Invisible thread
- [ ] 2" hook and loop tape, 1" wide
- [ ] Anti-fray solution
- [ ] Fabric adhesive

- [ ] All-purpose threads to match fabrics
- [ ] Buttons
- [ ] 1 package black rickrack trim
- [ ] Craft adhesive
- [ ] Quilt basting spray

TOOLS

- [ ] Basic sewing supplies
- [ ] Rotary cutting supplies
- [ ] Presser feet: ¼" foot, darning foot

Instructions
Please read all of the instructions before beginning this project. Refer to Chapter 1: Getting Started for detailed information on tools and techniques. All seams are ¼" wide; use a ¼" foot for accurate seams.

Cut the Materials

FROM	CUT	FOR
Beige print	1 square, 3½" x 3½"	Center block
Medium purple print	2 strips, 1¾" x 18"	Block
Black print	2 strips, 1¾" x 18"	Block
	2 strips, 3" x 18"	Handles
Medium blue print	4 strips, 1¾" x 18"*	Block
	3 squares, 11" x 11"	Tote back and backing/lining
	As needed, bias strips 2¼" wide	Bias binding
Batting	2 squares, 11" x 11"	Tote front and back
	2 strips, 1¼" x 18"	Handles

Cutting four medium blue strips will avoid piecing.

Make the Block

1 Sew the 1¾" medium purple strip, right sides together, to one side of the 3½" beige square. Cut the strip off after making the seam. Press toward the strip. Add the remaining strips the same way, in numeric order as shown.

Add the strips in numeric order.

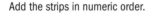

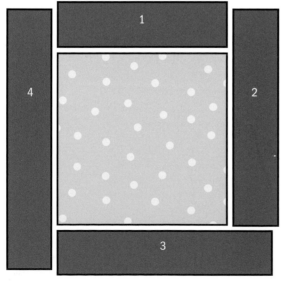

2 Sew the 1¾" black strips around the block in the same manner as the strips were added in Step 1. Press all seams toward the strip.

3 Sew the 1¾" medium blue strips around the block in the same manner as the strips were added in Step 1. Press all seams toward the strip.

• • • • •

Quilt the Tote Front Block and Back

1 Lay the 11" x 11" medium blue backing/lining square face down. Spray both sides of the 11" x 11" batting square, and lay it on top of the backing/lining square. Place the pieced block right side up on top of the batting. You may decide to hand quilt this tote for an authentic Amish look.

2 Using the darning foot, a matching thread in the bobbin and invisible thread for the topstitching, free-motion quilt the layers together. See Getting Started for details.

3 Repeat Steps 1 and 2 for the tote back.

4 Trim the front and back tote pieces to 10" square; use a 12" square ruler for accuracy.

• • • • •

Add the Rickrack

1 Beginning at the top right side of the block, hold the rickrack with your hands as you position the edge of the rickrack to the raw edge of the block as shown.

2 Sew down the center of the rickrack. Turn the corners carefully, with your needle in the down position. Backstitch at the beginning and end of your stitching.

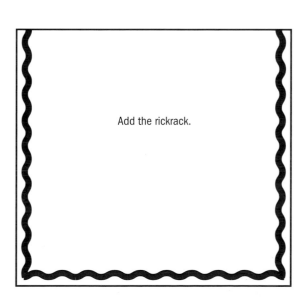

Add the rickrack.

Sew the Tote Together

1 With right sides together, sew the front and back tote pieces together. Zigzag the raw edges to secure the threads.

2 With right sides together, fold the tote corner so that the side seam meets up with the bottom seam of the tote. You will need to peek inside of the tote to make sure that the seams line up. Pin the pieces together to keep them in place.

3 Sew 1¼" from the corner. Zigzag next to the seam and cut off the extra fabric. See Getting Started for details.

4 Turn the tote right side out in preparation to add the binding.

Add the Binding

1 Sew together enough 2¼"-wide medium blue bias binding strips to go around the top edge of the tote. See Getting Started for details.

2 Sew the binding to the top edge of the tote. See Getting Started for details.

Add the Quilt Buttons

1 Lay the buttons on the front of the tote in the quilt block pattern.

2 Use craft adhesive to glue the buttons onto the center of the tote block, or, sew them on by hand.

3 Lay the bag flat to dry.

Make the Handles

1 Press under ¼" on one of the 18" sides for each 3" x 18" black fabric strip.

2 Position a strip of batting on the inside center of each 3" x 18" black fabric strip. See Getting Started for details. My tote ended up with four rows of stitching due to the position of the fold when I sewed the first row of stitching.

3 Cut the ends of the handles straight. Apply anti-fray solution to the cut ends.

4 Sew the handles to the inside top edge of the tote, 2" from the side seam. Stitch in the ditch of the binding on the front of the tote as shown.

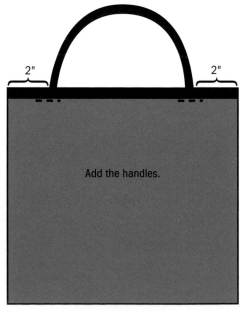

2"   2"

Add the handles.

Add the Hook and Loop Tape

1 Cut a ½" x 1½" piece of hook and loop tape. Keep the two pieces of the hook and loop tape together.

2 Use fabric adhesive to glue the hook and loop tape into the inside center of the tote. Lay the tote flat to dry to ensure that the tape pieces will be centered.

The COTTAGE Tote

YOU'LL WANT TO take this pretty yet practical tote everywhere you go! The Cottage Tote is the perfect partner to take to a quilting class or scrapbooking workshop; it's large enough to hold anything from an album to the 12"-square envelopes used to store pieced quilt blocks. The hearts were hand appliquéd, but you may want to use the blanket stitch on your sewing machine. I call this bag the Cottage Tote because the fabric colors give it a cottage feel. If cottage style isn't your taste, try another combination of colors to suit your style, such as black and white, red and blue or purple and yellow. You may have to have one in every color! Finished size: 14" x 15".

YOU WILL NEED

FABRIC

- ½ yd. gold print 1 (block, zipper panel backing/lining, front and back backing/lining)
- ⅛ yd. gold print 2 (border)
- ¼ yd. gold print 3 (side panel, side panel backing/lining, zipper tab)
- ⅛ yd. medium-green print 1 (block)
- ¼ yd. medium-green print 2 (handles, borders, heart appliqué)
- Scrap medium-green print 3 (borders, heart appliqué)
- Scrap medium-green print 4 (heart appliqué)
- Scrap medium-green print 5 (heart appliqué)
- ½ yd. medium-pink print 1 (zipper panel/tote back)
- ⅛ yd. medium-pink print 2 (block)
- ⅛ yd. medium-pink print 3 (borders)
- Scrap medium-pink print 4 (heart appliqué)
- Scrap medium-pink print 5 (heart appliqué)
- ⅛ yd. cream fabric (border)

NOTIONS

- ¼ yd. lightweight fusible web
- Embroidery floss in gold, green and pink
- All-purpose threads to match fabrics
- Anti-fray solution
- 18" zipper to match fabrics
- ⅓ yd. green satin ribbon to match tote, ¼" wide
- Hand embroidery needle
- Quilt basting spray

TOOLS

- Basic sewing supplies
- Presser feet: ¼" foot, walking foot, zipper foot
- Rotary cutting tools

PATTERNS

Heart Pattern (inside pattern insert)

Instructions

Please read all of the instructions before beginning this project. Refer to Chapter 1: Getting Started for detailed information on tools and techniques. All seams are ¼" wide; use a ¼" foot for accurate seams.

Cut the Materials

FROM	CUT	FOR
Gold print 1	6 squares, 3⅜" x 3⅜" 2 strips, 1¾" x 16¼" 2 rectangles, 15" x 17"	Block Zipper panel backing/lining Tote front and back lining/backing
Gold print 2	1 strip, 2" x 16¼"	Border
Gold print 3	2 strips, 1½" x 2¾" 2 strips, 3" x 45"*	Zipper tab Side panel
Medium-green print 1	4 squares, 3" x 3" 2 squares, 3⅜ " x 3⅜"	Block Block
Medium-green print 2	2 strips, 3½" x 24" 2 strips, 2" x 10¼"	Handles Border
Medium-green print 3	2 rectangles, 2" x 3"	Border
Medium-pink print 1	4 squares, 3⅜" x 3⅜"	Block
Medium-pink print 2	2 strips, 2" x 10¼"**	Border
Medium-pink print 3	2 strips, 1¾" x 16¼" 1 rectangle, 15" x 17"	Zipper panel Tote back
Cream	1 strip, 3½" x 13⅜"	Block
Batting	2 rectangles, 15" x 17" 1 strip, 3" x 45" 2 strips, 1" x 24" 2 strips, 1¾" x 16¼"	Tote front and back Tote side panel Handles Zipper panels

* *This is an approximate length; the block size may vary.*

** *This cut may need to be adjusted, as all blocks will be different. Measure your block after it is finished, and cut the rectangles to that length.*

****Hearts will be cut later from medium-green 1, 3, 4 & 5 and medium-pink 4 & 5*

Tip

Use sticky notes to label the pieces you cut; it makes it much easier to find the right piece when you're ready to sew!

• • • • •

Make the Block

1 Draw a diagonal pencil line across the six 3⅜" gold 1 squares.

2 With right sides together, sew two 3⅜" gold 1 squares and two 3⅜" medium-green 1 squares together. Sew ¼" away from the pencil line as shown.

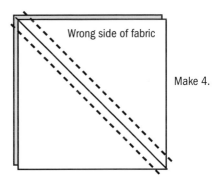

Wrong side of fabric

Make 4.

3 Cut across the pencil line to make four half-square triangles. Press toward the green, and set it aside.

4 Repeat Steps 2 and 3 for the remaining four 3⅜" gold 1 squares and the four 3⅜" medium-pink 1 squares. Press toward the pink. You will end up with eight half-square triangles.

5 Position all of the half-square triangles and the four 3" medium-green 1 squares as shown.

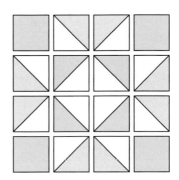

6 Sew the squares, right sides together, in Rows 1 through 4 in the order shown. Press the seams in Row 1 and Row 3 to the right, press the seams in Row 2 and Row 4 to the left.

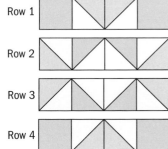

Row 1

Row 2

7 Sew the rows together as shown.

Row 3

Row 4

8 Sew the 2" x 10¼" medium-pink 2 strips, right sides together, to both sides of the block as shown. Press to the pink.

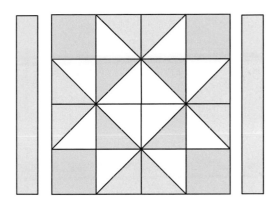

9 Sew the 2" x 10¼" medium-green 2 strips, right sides together, to the pink rectangles as shown. Press toward the green.

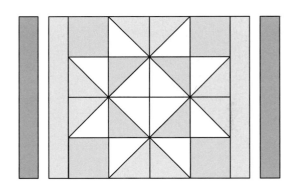

10 Sew the 2" x 16¼" gold 2 strip, right sides together, to the bottom of the block as shown. Press toward the gold.

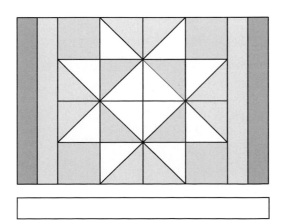

11 Sew the 2" x 3" medium-green 3 rectangles, right sides together, to the 3½" x 13⅜" cream rectangle. Press toward the green.

12 Sew the strip created in Step 11 to the top of the block as shown. Press toward the strip.

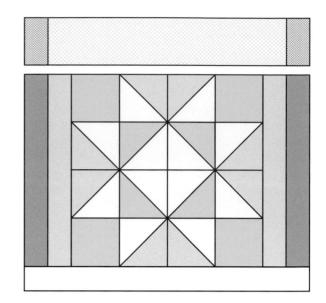

> **Option** If you wish to machine appliqué the hearts to the cream rectangle, you may want to do so now for ease of handling. If so, skip the to section Appliqué the Hearts, and substitute colored threads and a machine blanket stitch for the embroidery floss and hand blanket stitch.

Appliqué the Hearts

1 Use the Heart Pattern on the pattern insert to trace six heart shapes onto fusible web. Cut outside the lines ¼".

2 Fuse one heart shape to six different fabric scraps. For this tote, the following fabrics were used: medium-green 2, medium-green 3, medium-green 4, medium-green 5, medium-pink 4 and medium-pink 5.

3 Position the six different hearts on the 3½" x 13⅜" cream rectangle on the front of the tote. Leave enough room for a ¼" seam above the hearts.

4 Use colored embroidery floss to blanket stitch around each of the hearts. See Getting Started for details. Use yellow floss for two of the green hearts, pink floss for two of the green hearts and green floss for the two pink hearts.

Quilt the Tote Front

1 Lay the 15" x 17" gold 1 rectangle face down. Lay one 15" x 17" batting rectangle that has been sprayed on both sides with basting spray on top of the gold 1 rectangle. Lay the tote front, right side up, on top of the batting.

2 Use matching thread to quilt in the ditch along the seam lines.

3 Trim all of the edges straight.

> **Option** You may choose to use pink embroidery floss to hand quilt in the cream rectangle, ¼" away from the seams.

Quilt the Tote Back

1 Lay the 15" x 17" medium-pink 3 rectangle face down. Lay one 15" x 17" batting rectangle that has been sprayed on both sides with basting spray on top of the gold 1 rectangle. Lay the tote back face up on top of the batting.

2 Use matching thread to quilt a 1½"-wide vertical straight pattern as shown.

3 Cut the tote back to the same size as the tote front. Set tote front and tote back pieces aside.

Add the Side Panels

1. Lay the 3" x 45" gold 2 strip face down. Lay the 3" x 45" batting strip that has been sprayed on both sides with basting spray on top of the gold 2 strip. Lay the second 3" x 45" gold 2 strip face up on top of the batting.

2. Sew along both edges and down the center to quilt the piece and keep the layers together.

3. Sew the side panel, right sides together, along three sides of the tote front. Backstitch at the beginning and end of the seam. Zigzag the raw edges. Cut off the extra side panel, if necessary.

4. Repeat Step 3 for the tote back as shown.

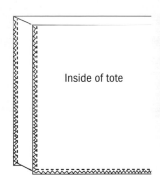

Inside of tote

Make the Zipper Panel

1. Lay the 1¾" x 16¼" gold 1 strip face down. Lay the 1¾" x 16¼" batting strip that has been sprayed on both sides with basting spray on top of the gold 1 strip. Lay the 1¾" x 16¼" medium-pink 3 strip face up on top of the batting.

2. With a walking foot, sew along both edges and down the center to quilt and keep the layers together.

3. Repeat Steps 1 and 2 for the remaining zipper panel piece.

4. Add the zipper to the zipper panel pieces. See Getting Started for details.

Make the Handles

1. Using the 1" x 24" batting strips and 3½" x 24" medium-green 1 strips, make the handles. See Getting Started for details.

2. Apply anti-fray solution to the ends of the handles. Set the handles aside to dry.

3. Sew the handles, right sides together, to the tote front and back so they are 4" from the right and left edges; match the raw edges together.

Add the Zipper Tab

1. Press under ¼" along both 2¾" sides of the 1½" x 2¾" gold 2 rectangles.

2. Press the rectangles in half again. Topstitch along both edges of each tab.

3. Sew the tabs to each edge of the zipper panel as shown.

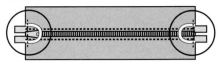

Add the Zipper Panel

1. Unzip the zipper so it will be easier to turn the piece right side out. Sew the zipper panel, right sides together, to the tote. Zigzag the raw edges.

2. Tie a ¼" x 5" piece of satin ribbon to the zipper pull. Apply anti-fray solution to both ends of the ribbon.

The *Y*ORKSHIRE Tote

THIS QUICK-TO-MAKE TOTE is the perfect size for practically everything! It's the perfect bag to hold your makeup or hold small items inside your purse, or as a bag to stash sewing supplies for class or photos for a scrapbook page. For a different look, dress this bag up in velvets and silks to create a classy evening clutch to hold all of your incidentals. This versatile little bag is perfect for so many things, you'll want to make one for all of these uses, plus plenty for family and friends, too. Finished size: 7" x 11".

YOU WILL NEED

FABRIC

- [ ] Scraps of six different gold, green, brown, cream and burgundy coordinating fabrics, each at least 3" square (block)
- [ ] ⅓ yd. coordinating green print 1 (tote back, handle, block)
- [ ] ⅓ yd. coordinating green print 2 (backing/lining, block)
- [ ] ⅛ yd. coordinating green print 3 (borders)

NOTIONS

- [ ] ¼ yd. 100 percent cotton batting
- [ ] Invisible thread
- [ ] 2 bronze eyelets, ¼" diameter
- [ ] Gilded eye pin used for beading
- [ ] Quilt basting spray

- [ ] All-purpose threads to match fabrics
- [ ] 12" camel-colored zipper
- [ ] 1 package beads
- [ ] Anti-fray solution

TOOLS

- [ ] Basic sewing supplies
- [ ] Rotary cutting tools
- [ ] Presser feet: ¼" foot, walking foot, zipper foot

- [ ] 3-in-1 beading tool
- [ ] ¼" eyelet tool

Instructions Please read all of the instructions before beginning this project. Refer to Chapter 1: Getting Started for detailed information on tools and techniques. All seams are ¼" wide; use a ¼" foot for accurate seams.

Cut the Materials

FROM	CUT	FOR
Each of the six scraps	1 square, 2¾" x 2¾"	Block
Green print 1	1 rectangle, 8½" x 12½"	Tote back
	1 strip, 1½" x 18½"	Handle
	1 square, 2¾" x 2¾"	Block
Green print 2	2 rectangles, 8½" x 12½"	Backing/lining
	1 strip, 2" x 45"	Border
	1 square, 2¾" x 2¾"	Block
Green print 3	1 strip, 2" x 45"	Border
Batting	2 rectangles, 8½" x 12½"	Tote front and back
	1 strip, ⅜" x 18½"	Handle

Make the Block

1 Randomly position the eight different 2¾" squares in a pleasing manner so there are four squares for Row 1 and four squares for Row 2.

2 Sew four squares, right sides together, in Row 1, as shown. Press to the left. Sew four squares, right sides together, in Row 2, as shown. Press to the right.

3 Sew Row 1, right sides together, to Row 2. Press the seam to one side.

4 Sew the 2" x 45" green strip to the four sides of the block. Note: You will sew the strip to one side at a time, then cut it and use the remainder for the next side. Sew one 2" green strip across the top, then sew one 2" green strip across the bottom. Press toward the strips. Sew one 2" green strip to the right side of the block, and then sew one 2" green strip to the left side of the block. Press toward the strips.

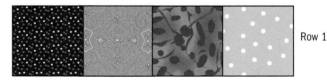

Row 1

Row 2

Quilt the Tote Front and Back

1 Lay the 8½" x 12½" green 2 backing/lining face down. Lay the 8½" x 12½" batting rectangle, which has been sprayed on both sides with basting spray, on top of the green 2 rectangle. Lay the tote front face up on top of the batting.

2 Use a walking foot to quilt a crisscross pattern over the tote front; cross over the intersections of the blocks approximately 1½" apart. You can place a measuring guide on your walking foot, or you can make crisscross markings with the white chalk pencil and the ¼" ruler.

3 Repeat Steps 1 and 2 for the tote back; use the 8½" x 12½" green 2 backing/lining, batting and the 8½" x 12½" green 1 tote back.

4 Trim both the front and back down to 7" x 11¼".

Add the Zipper

1 Use the zipper foot to sew the zipper, right sides together, to the raw edge of the tote front. Position the zipper so that the actual zipper is ¼" from the edge. See Getting Started for details.

2 Backstitch at the beginning and the end.

Make the Beaded Zipper Pull

1 Pick three beads from the package of beads. I chose three that were different colors and shapes.

2 Thread the beads onto the eye pin. Use the beading tool to cut off the end of the eye pin, but leave about ¼" of the pin to be used to make a loop.

3 Use the beading tool to make a loop. Secure the loop to the hole in the zipper pull.

Sew the Tote Together

1 Unzip the zipper to make it easier to turn the tote right side out. With right sides together, sew the three sides of the tote together. Backstitch at each end.

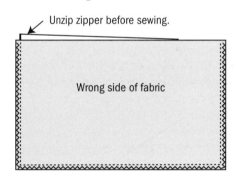

Unzip zipper before sewing.

Wrong side of fabric

2 Zigzag the raw edges as shown.

3 Before turning the tote right side out, make the purse corners. See Getting Started for details.

4 Sew across the layers, 1" from the purse corner. Zigzag next to the seam. Trim off the extra fabric. Repeat for the other corner.

5 Turn the tote right side out.

Add the Eyelets and the Handle

1 Position an eyelet on the side edge of the bag, near the zipper opening; it will be approximately ¼" from the side of the tote and the zipper. You will be putting in two eyelets, one on the front and one on the back of the tote, and they need to line up with each other so the handle will pull through as shown.

2 Use the eyelet tool to cut a small hole for each eyelet; use the eyelet as a guide. The hole won't be very big; otherwise the eyelet won't stay in place. The fabric will stretch over the eyelet piece.

3 Install the eyelets; follow the manufacturer's instructions.

4 Using the ⅜" x 18½" batting strip and the 1½" x 18½" green 1 strip, make the handle. Refer to Getting Started for details.

5 Apply anti-fray solution to the ends of the handle; set the handle aside to allow it to dry.

6 Thread the handle through the eyelets, and tie the ends in a knot.

CHAPTER 3

Working Bags

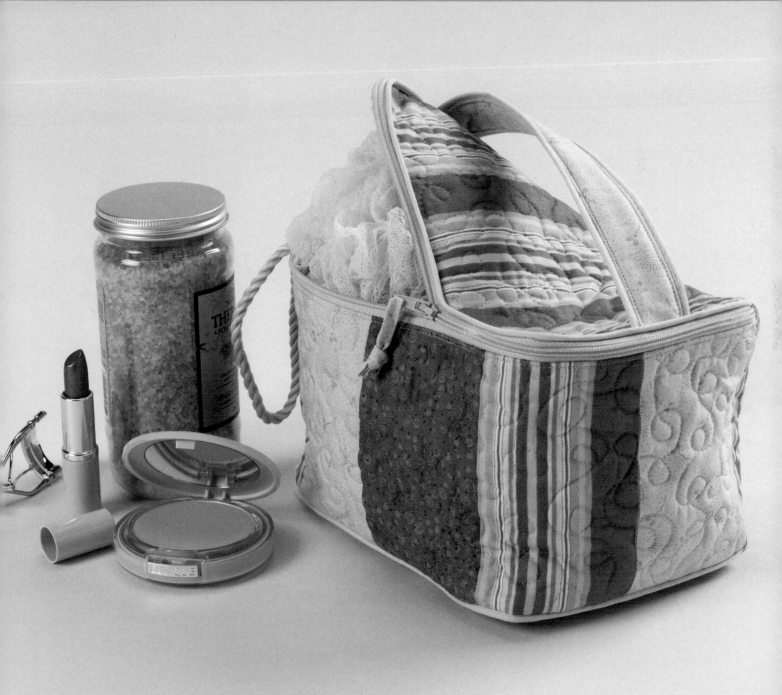

Erin's CLUTCH

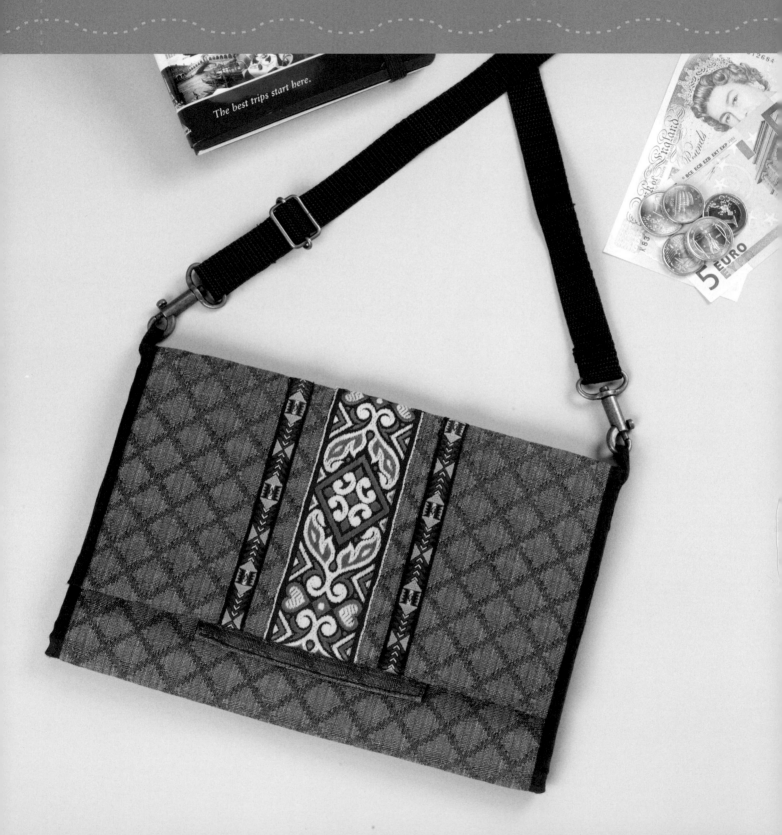

THIS LITTLE CLUTCH is like a wallet. There are many places to keep all of the important things that you need for going out or traveling. A zippered section has plenty of room for bills, coins and a pen. There is pocket section for your driver's license, and another to hold several credit cards. There is even a small pocket for business cards, as well as an area to hold pieces of paper for notes. Finished size: 6½" x 9¼".

YOU WILL NEED

FABRIC

- ½ yd. black fabric (lining, pocket)
- ⅓ yd. red decorator print/solid (cover, pocket)

NOTIONS

- 1½ yd. black webbing, ¾" wide (strap)
- ⅓ yd. red/green/cream trim, 1¾" wide (cover)
- 9" black zipper
- All-purpose threads to match fabrics
- Anti-fray solution
- 2 antique gold ¾" swivel rings
- White chalk pencil
- ¼ yd. stiff, fusible interfacing
- Quilt basting spray

- 1 yd. black/gold trim, ½" wide (cover, pockets)
- ⅛ yd. woven, iron-on interfacing (pocket stabilizer)
- 1 package black twill tape, ½" wide
- 12" clear ruler
- 2 antique gold ¾" magnetic closures
- 1 antique gold ¾" adjustable strap slide
- 3 yd. ³⁄₁₆"-wide fusible web tape
- 1 heavy, clear sheet protector (pocket)

TOOLS

- Basic sewing supplies
- Rotary cutting tools
- Presser feet: ¼" foot, zipper foot

Instructions Please read all of the instructions before beginning this project. Refer to Chapter 1: Getting Started for detailed information on tools and techniques. All seams are ¼" wide; use a ¼" foot for accurate seams.

Cut the Materials

FROM	CUT	FOR
Red	1 rectangle, 9" x 18"	Clutch cover
	1 rectangle, 5" x 9"	Zipper pocket
	1 rectangle, 4" x 5"	Small Pocket
Black	1 rectangle, 9" x 15½"	Lining
	2 rectangles, 4¼" x 9"	Large pocket
	1 rectangle, 3" x 5"	Small pocket
	1 rectangle, 5" x 9"	Zipper pocket lining

Make the Cover

1 Cut two 7" pieces of the ½"-wide black/gold trim and one 7" piece of the 1¾"-wide red/green/cream trim.

2 Find the center of the 9" side of the 9" x 18" red clutch cover piece by folding the 9" side in half and marking it with a pin.

3 Measure vertically 6¼" from the center pin; mark that spot with another pin. Use the clear ruler and chalk pencil to draw a line from the center pin to the second pin mark as shown.

4 Draw chalk lines 1½" from each side of the center chalk line. These lines mark the lines you'll use to sew on the trim.

5 With right sides together, pin the 1¾"-wide trim to the top of the chalk lines. Center the trim over the line as shown.

6 With right sides together, pin the pieces of ½"-wide trim to the remaining chalk lines.

7 Sew ¼" from the raw edge, backstitching at each end.

8 Press the trim over to the clutch. Pin the trim down; make sure it is straight.

9 Use matching thread to sew along both edges of the trim as shown below.

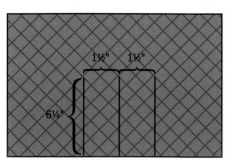
Make the chalk lines.

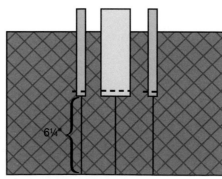
Pin the trim.

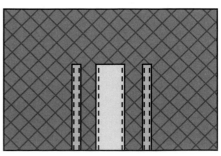
Sew the trim.

Add the Lining and the Magnetic Snaps (Male Part)

1 Cut a 1½" x 9" piece of woven, iron-on interfacing.

2 Press the interfacing to the wrong side of the clutch flap, along the raw edge as shown.

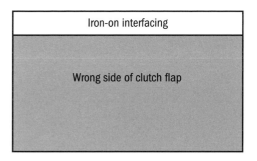

Iron-on interfacing

Wrong side of clutch flap

3 Press 1⅜" of the purse flap toward the wrong side.

4 Mark the positions for the snaps with a pen "dot." The dots will be 1⅛" from the edge of the black trim and ¾" from the folded and pressed edge as shown.

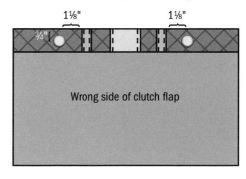

1⅛"   1⅛"
¾"

Wrong side of clutch flap

5 Cut a 9" x 18" piece of stiff, fusible interfacing. If the stiff, fusible interfacing is too small, you can zigzag a piece together to make up the difference, and then cut to size.

6 Position the stiff, fusible interfacing on the wrong side of the red print. Secure it with pins; do NOT fuse it.

7 Sew the 9" x 15½" black rectangle, right sides together, to the purse flap.

8 To cut accurate slits for the snap clasps, place the frame of the snap onto the pen mark. Mark the two slits with a pen, and remove the frame. Put a straight pin at the end of the slit. Use a seam ripper to poke into the fabric, opposite of the slit. Push the seam ripper until it cuts through the fabric to the pin. The pin will stop the seam ripper from going beyond the pen mark.

9 Attach the male part of the snap; follow the manufacturer's directions. You will be attaching the snaps through the stiff, fusible interfacing for strength. For a more secure snap, fold the flaps of the snap inward rather than outward.

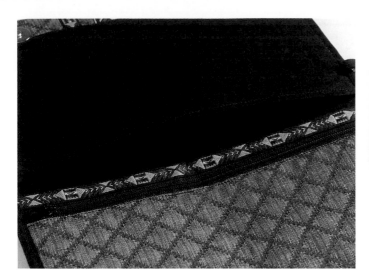

• • • • •

Make the Large Pocket

1 Cut a 4¼" x 9" piece of woven, iron-on interfacing.

2 Press the interfacing to the wrong side of one of the 4¼" x 9" black large-pocket pieces.

3 With right sides together, sew the interfaced piece to the remaining 4¼" x 9" black large-pocket piece. Leave an opening to turn the piece right side out. Trim the corners to remove bulk.

4 Turn the pocket right side out, and press. Topstitch one of the 9" sides ¼" from the edge.

5 Sew the large pocket onto the black lining fabric, without sewing through the stiff interfacing, so it is ½" below the snap on the clutch flap. Stitch along the three sides as shown.

• • • • •

Make the Zipper Pouch

1 Lay the 5" x 9" red rectangle, wrong sides together, on the 5" x 9" black rectangle, treating them as one piece of fabric.

2 Use the zipper foot to attach the zipper, right sides together, to the 9" side of the 5" x 9" red rectangle; position the zipper ¼" from the side. Zigzag the seam and the bottom raw edge.

3 Pin the pocket to the black lining only, 6½" from the top edge of the purse. Avoid sewing through the stiff, fusible interfacing.

4 Press under the bottom edge of the pocket ½" and pin in place. Sew across the zipper and the three edges; sew close to the edge.

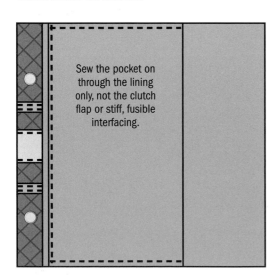

Sew the pocket on through the lining only, not the clutch flap or stiff, fusible interfacing.

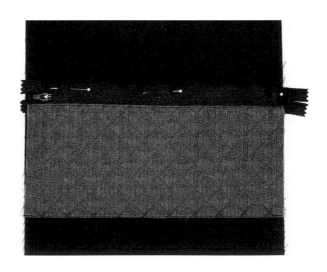

Make the ID and Credit Card Pocket

1 Cut a 3¼" x 9" piece of sheet protector.

2 Press a 9" piece of twill tape in half, lengthwise. Wrap the twill tape over the 9" edge of the sheet protector, and sew it to the sheet protector using black thread.

3 Baste the pocket onto the black lining fabric only, along the three sides just below the zipper pouch. Leave a ⅛" space. Cover the plastic with a strip of paper, so that the plastic will move through the sewing machine as you sew. Align the paper to the edge of the sheet protector.

4 Press a 3¼" piece of black twill tape in half, lengthwise. Sew the twill tape vertically down the center of the pocket as shown.

5 Sew a 9" piece of black/gold trim to the bottom of the pocket as shown below. Avoid pressing the plastic sheet as you iron.

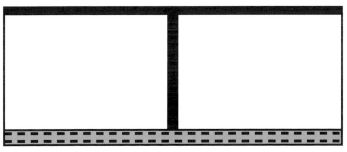

Add the trim.

Add the Magnetic Snaps (Female Part)

1 Fold the clutch as you would to close it. With two pins in a crisscross pattern, mark the point where the male snap rests on the clutch as shown.

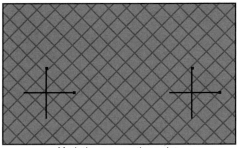

Mark the snap resting point.

2 Make a pen dot at the crossing point.

3 Place the frame of the snap onto the pen mark. Mark the two slits with a pen, and remove the frame. Put a straight pin at the end of the slit. Use a seam ripper to poke into the fabric, opposite of the slit. Push the seam ripper until it cuts through the fabric to the pin. The pin will stop the seam ripper from going beyond the pen mark.

4 Follow the manufacturer's directions to attach the snaps. You will be attaching the snaps through the stiff interfacing. The lining and the cover should not be sewn together yet; they should still be separate pieces.

Make the Small Pocket

1 With right sides together, sew the 4" x 5" red rectangle and the 3" x 5" black rectangle along the 5" side. Press the seam toward the black.

2 Topstitch close to the edge on the black fabric as shown.

Sew the pocket.

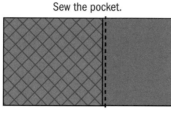

Wrong side of black fabric

3 Sew the pocket right sides together; match the end of the black to the end of the red. Leave an opening to turn right side out, and trim the corners as shown.

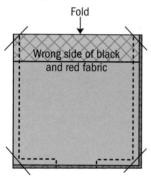

Fold

Wrong side of black and red fabric

4 Turn the pocket right side out. Press all of the edges.

5 Topstitch across the top with two rows of stitching that are ¼" apart.

6 Position the small pocket onto the underflap of the clutch. Center the pocket between the snaps and ¾" from the raw edge.

7 Stitch around the three sides of the pocket, backstitching at each end as shown,

Make the Handle Loops

1 Cut a 6" piece of twill tape, and press it in half lengthwise.

2 Sew the trim closed along the open side.

3 Cut the segment in half to make two 3" pieces, and apply anti-fray solution to all of the ends. Set the pieces aside to dry.

4 Fold one 3" piece in half to make a loop. Position the loop along the edge of the purse, 4¾" from the top of the purse. Sew the loop to the inside of the purse as shown.

5 Repeat Step 4 for the second loop.

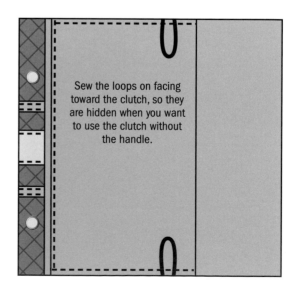

Sew the loops on facing toward the clutch, so they are hidden when you want to use the clutch without the handle.

Bind the Purse

1 Cut all of the edges straight.

2 Baste all of the layers, wrong sides together. Make the basting stitch less than ¼" from the sides.

3 Cut enough twill tape to go around the purse to cover two long sides, one short side and have 1" remaining. It should be enough to sew along the two long sides and one short side, plus 1".

4 Use black thread to sew the twill tape onto the red side of the clutch. Overlap the edge of the clutch evenly with the twill tape. Leave ½" of tape at the beginning and at the end to tuck the tape under.

5 Apply two small pieces of fusible web tape at the beginning and end of the twill tape. Press the ½" end or "tale" of twill tape onto the small fusible web tape. (This will clean up the ends)

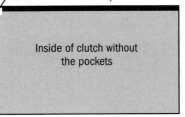

Piece of fusible web tape.

Inside of clutch without the pockets

6 Apply fusible web tape close to the edge onto the wrong side along all three edges of the twill tape. Remove the paper. Fold the tape over, and press all around the clutch. NOTE: Use the very tip of the iron to carefully press only the twill tape at the edge of the plastic sheet protector. Avoid burning the plastic.

7 Sew the twill tape ¼" from the edge on the outside (red side) of the clutch. Sewing from the outside of the clutch will ensure that the stitching won't show where you don't want it.

Make the Webbing Strap

1 Sew one end of the webbing to the center loop on the ¾" slider. Turn the end under by ¼" and sew in place.

2 Thread the other end of the webbing through one of the ¾" swivel rings and then through the slider to hold the swivel ring inside of the loop.

3 Sew the remaining end of the webbing onto the remaining ¾" swivel ring, and turn the end under by ¼".

4 Hook the swivel rings to the loops on the clutch.

Tip

This clutch also can be used without the loops. When the strap is detached, the loops will stay inside of the clutch.

The *Messenger* Bag

THE MESSENGER-STYLE BAG has been around for a long time. A lot of students use these bags because the strap is nice to carry over the shoulder and body. This version also makes a great professional accessory to carry things back and forth from the office; multiple pockets make it a snap to stay organized. To make The Messenger even better, make the coordinating Luggage Tag and Aubrey's Tote featured in this chapter. Finished size: 11" x 14".

YOU WILL NEED

FABRIC

- ½ yd. designer fabric (bag, tote bottom insert)
- ½ yd. coordinating green fabric (flap, pocket lining)
- ¾ yd. burgundy print (flap, lining, strap, outside pocket)
- 1 yd. muslin
- ½ yd. black print (flap, binding)
- ¼ yd. gold print (flap, inside pocket)

NOTIONS

- ½ yd. 100 percent cotton batting
- 1/8 yd. stiff, fusible interfacing (tote bottom insert)
- Invisible thread
- 1¾ yd. black webbing, 1¾" wide
- 2 side-release black plastic buckles, 1" size
- Quilt basting spray
- ¼ yd. woven, iron-on interfacing
- All-purpose threads to match fabrics
- 12" black metal zipper
- 2 swivel hooks, 1¾" size
- 1 yd. black webbing, 1" wide
- Tote bag strap sliding shoulder pad, optional

TOOLS

- Basic sewing supplies
- Rotary cutting tools
- Presser feet: ¼" foot, walking foot, darning foot, zipper foot

Instructions
Please read all of the instructions before beginning this project. Refer to Chapter 1: Getting Started for detailed information on tools and techniques. All seams are ¼" wide; use a ¼" foot for accurate seams.

Cut the Materials

FROM	CUT	FOR
Designer fabric	2 rectangles, 12" x 15"	Tote front and back
	1 strip, 4" x 44"	Tote side panel
	2 rectangles, 3" x 13½"	Tote bottom insert
Muslin	2 rectangles, 12" x 15"	Front and back backing
	1 strip, 4" x 44"	Side panel backing
	1 square, 6" x 6"	Strap cover backing
Green fabric	1 strip, 2⅜" x 7½"	Flap pocket
	2 strips, 1¼" x 7½"	Flap pocket
	1 strip, 1¼" x 11¼"	Flap pocket
	1 rectangle, 5¾" x 11¼"	Flap pocket lining
	1 rectangle, 2¼" x 11¼"	Flap pocket lining
	2 squares, 13" x 13"	Purse flap
Gold print	1 strip, 2⅜" x 7½"	Flap pocket
	2 rectangles, 5½" x 10½"	Lining pocket
Burgundy print	1 strip, 2⅜" x 7½"	Flap pocket
	2 rectangles, 11½" x 14"	Tote lining
	1 strip, 3½" x 44"	Tote side lining
	1 square, 6" x 6"	Strap covers
	2 rectangles, 9¾" x 12"	Back pocket and lining
Black print	2 strips, 2⅜" x 7½"	Flap pocket
	2 strips, 2" x 11"	Flap pocket
	Bias strips as needed, 2¼" wide	Binding
Iron-on interfacing	1 rectangle, 5½" x 10½"	Lining pocket
Stiff, fusible interfacing	1 rectangle, 2½" x 13"	Tote bottom insert
Batting	2 rectangles, 12" x 15"	Tote front and back
	1 strip, 4" x 44"	Tote side panel
	1 square, 13" x 13"	Purse flap
	1 rectangle, 9¾" x 12"	Back pocket
	1 square, 6" x 6"	Strap covers

Tip

Label each piece. Use sticky notes or pin notes to each piece, which will make it easy to pick out what you need.

Quilt the Front, Back and Side Panels

1 Lay the 12" x 15" muslin piece face down. Lay the 12" x 15" batting rectangle, which has been sprayed on both sides with basting spray, on top of the muslin. Lay the 12" x 15" decorator print rectangle face up on top of the batting.

2 Quilt as desired. I machine quilted this tote with a 1"-wide crisscross design. Use the walking foot with the guide positioned 1" from the needle. Draw a 45-degree line with a chalk pencil and ruler to follow the first line of quilting.

3 Repeat Step 2 with the remaining 12" x 15" muslin and decorator rectangles as shown.

4 Repeat Step 2 with the 4" x 44" strips of muslin, batting and decorator fabric.

5 Cut the front and back rectangles down to 11½" x 14". Cut the side panel strips down to 3½" x 44". Set aside.

Make the Flap Pocket

1 With right sides together, sew each of the 2⅜" x 7½" strips along the 7½" sides in the color order shown. Press the seams to one side.

Sew the pocket strips together.

2 Sew a green 1¼" x 7½" strip to each side of the above piece. Press the seams toward the center.

3 Sew a green 1¼" x 11¼" strip across the bottom of the above piece. Press seams toward the center as shown and cut off any excess.

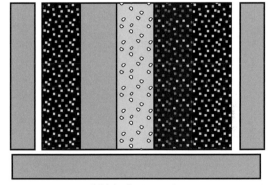

Add the bottom strip.

4 Cut a piece of muslin and batting 2" larger than the flap pocket.

5 Lay the muslin piece cut in Step 4 face down. Spray both sides of the batting piece cut in Step 4 with temporary spray adhesive, and lay it on top of the muslin piece. Lay the flap pocket face up on the batting.

6 Quilt as desired. I machine quilted the flap pocket with a loopy design.

7 Trim and square up the edges; remove the extra batting and muslin.

Add the Zipper to the Pocket Flap

1 Cut 2¼" off the top of the pocket flap as shown. Set it aside.

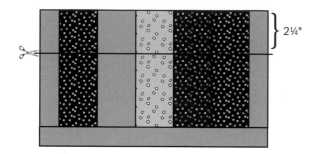

2 Use a zipper foot to sew the 12" black zipper, right sides together, to the bottom flap.

3 Sew the 2¼"-wide top pocket flap to the opposite side of the zipper; match the strips of fabric up to each other, and pin the strips in place.

Sew the Flap Pocket Lining

1 Pin and sew the right side of the 2¼" x 11¼" green pocket lining to the wrong side of the zipper edge as shown.

2 Press the lining toward the flap. Pin the edges together and baste in place.

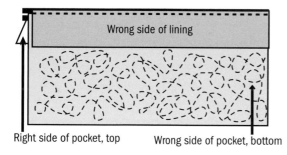

Right side of pocket, top   Wrong side of pocket, bottom

3 Repeat Steps 1 and 2 with the 5¾" x 11¼" green pocket lining.

4 Topstitch on the right side of the pocket, next to the zipper. Set aside.

Make the Purse Flap

1 Lay one 13" green square face down. Spray both sides of the 13" batting square with temporary adhesive, and lay it on top of the green square. Lay a second 13" green square face up on top of the batting.

2 Quilt the fabric in a loopy design. Cut the quilted flap down to an 11" square.

3 Position the flap pocket onto the bottom edge of the flap. Pin it in place, and baste around the edges.

4 Fold the 2" x 11" black strip in half lengthwise, with wrong sides together.

5 Sew right sides together, to the top edge of the pocket as shown.

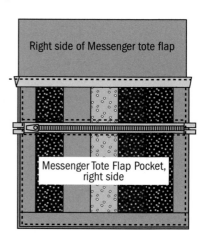

7 Flip the strip over, and topstitch it down close to the edge.

8 Carefully trim the zipper to the edge of the purse flap. Do not unzip the zipper, or you will lose the zipper pull.

9 Sew a piece of 2¼"-wide black bias tape around three sides of the flap as shown. Turn the bias tape over, and hand sew the folded edge to the back side of the flap to encase the raw edge of the pocket. Press lightly. See Getting Started for details.

Add the bias tape.

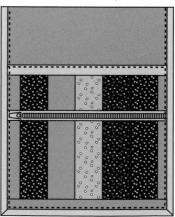

Make the Back Pocket

1 Lay a 9¾" x 12" burgundy rectangle face down. Spray both sides of a 9¾" x 12" batting rectangle with quilt basting spray, and place it on top of the burgundy fabric rectangle. Place a 9¾" x 12" rectangle of burgundy fabric face up on top of the batting.

2 Quilt the layers together with a loopy design. See Getting Started for details.

3 Trim all of the edges to straighten the piece.

Bind and Sew the Back Pocket to the Tote

1 Sew enough 2¼"-wide black bias binding strips to go around the back pocket. See Getting Started for details.

2 Bind all four sides of the back pocket.

3 Sew the pocket onto the back of the bag, approximately 1½" from the bag's top edge as shown; leave the top edge open. Stitch in the ditch, and then sew another row of stitching along the edge of the binding.

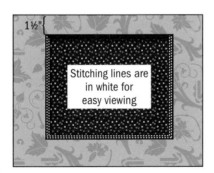

1½"

Stitching lines are in white for easy viewing

Make the Lining Pocket

1 Iron a 5½" x 10½" rectangle of woven, iron-on interfacing to the wrong side of one 5½" x 10½" gold lining pocket.

2 Sew the two lining pocket pieces, right sides together; leave an opening to turn the pieces right side out.

3 Trim the corners, and turn the pocket right side out. Press.

4 Topstitch two rows across the 10" edge of the pocket; keep the rows ¼" apart.

5 Pin the pocket 4½" from the top of the tote back lining and approximately 2¼" from both sides.

6 Use matching thread in the bobbin and the needle to sew the pocket onto the tote back lining. Follow measurements for pocket placement and stitching lines as shown.

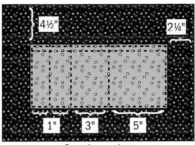

4½"   2¼"

1"   3"   5"

Sew the pocket.

Add the Purse Lining

1 Use temporary spray adhesive to baste one 11½" x 14" burgundy rectangle to the tote front, wrong sides together. Use temporary spray adhesive to baste one 11½" x 14" burgundy rectangle to the tote back, wrong sides together.

2 Use temporary spray adhesive to baste 3½" x 44" burgundy strip to tote side panel, wrong sides together.

Sew the Front Flap to the Tote

1 Position the front flap to the back of the tote, just above the top edge of the back pocket.

2 Sew across the raw edge. Sew a 2¼"-wide bias binding strip across the same seam; leave ¼" at each end of the strip.

3 Turn the ¼" ends of the strip inside. Fold over the binding, and sew along the folded edge of the binding as shown.

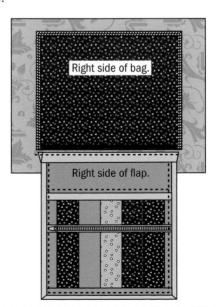

Right side of bag.

Right side of flap.

See instructions page 63 - Sew the Front and Back Together.

• • • • •

Make the Strap Covers

1 Lay the 6" muslin square face down. Spray basting spray on both sides of the 6" batting square, and lay the batting on top of the muslin square. Lay the 6" burgundy square face up on top of the batting.

2 Quilt the layers in a loopy design.

3 Cut the quilted layers into two 2⅜" squares.

• • • • •

Make the Strap

1 Apply anti-fray solution to both ends of the 1¾"-wide webbing.

2 Loop one end of the webbing around the center bar of the slider. Stitch it to secure it.

3 Thread one swivel hook to the opposite end of the webbing.

4 Thread the webbing back through the slider.

5 If desired, slip the sliding shoulder pad onto the webbing.

6 Loop the webbing through the other swivel hook, and sew the webbing to secure it.

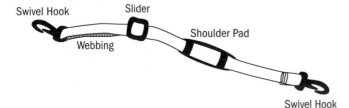

Swivel Hook · Slider · Webbing · Shoulder Pad · Swivel Hook

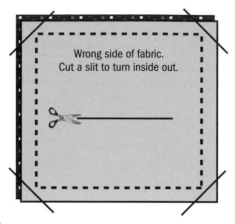

Wrong side of fabric.
Cut a slit to turn inside out.

4 Lay a quilted square, right sides together, with a 2⅜" burgundy square. Sew the squares together on all four sides. Trim the four corners, and cut a small slit in the back of the square as shown. Repeat for the second set of squares.

5 Turn the squares right side out. Press.

6 Make the straps using the sliders and swivel hooks as shown. See Getting Started for details.

7 Cut two 3" pieces of the 1¾"-wide black webbing. Thread the webbing through the D- or triangle ring. Pin it to hold it together. Tuck the webbing under the burgundy square, and sew it into place ½" below the top edge of the bag's side panel. Repeat for the other side.

Add the Side-Release Shoulder Strap Buckles

1 Cut two 2" pieces of the 1"-wide webbing. Thread one piece of 1"-wide webbing through the male part of each side-release buckle; follow the manufacturer's instructions.

2 Apply anti-fray solution to the ends of the webbing, and let it dry.

3 Sew the webbing and male part of the buckle underneath the front flap and just inside of the binding; position it so the side-release buckle is on the end.

4 Cut two 7" pieces of the 1"-wide webbing. Thread one piece of the 1"-wide webbing through the female part of each side-release buckle; follow the manufacturer's instructions.

5 Apply anti-fray solution to the ends of the webbing, and let it dry.

6 Attach the buckles, and pin the bottom edge of the webbing to the bottom edge of the front panel.

Sew the Front and Back Together

1. Find the center on all three sides of the front and back pieces. Find the center on both 44" sides of the side panel pieces. Mark each center with a pin.

2. With wrong sides together, sew the side panel to the front panel by matching the pins. Clip at the corners to allow easy turning of the side panels when you are sewing them together.

3. Repeat Step 2 for the back panel.

Bind the Front, Back and Top Edge of the Bag

1. Sew enough 2¼" black bias binding strips together to fit around the front, back and top edge of the bag.

2. Bind the front, back and top edge of the bag. See Getting Started for details.

Make the Tote Bottom Insert

1. Cover the 2½" x 13" piece of stiff, fusible interfacing with the two decorator 3" x 13½" rectangles, right sides out.

2. Iron the fabric onto each side of the stiff, fusible interfacing.

3. Zigzag around all four edges of the fabric-covered insert.

4. Place the insert in the bottom of the bag.

The LUGGAGE TAG

Name

Address

City

State

Phone

Zip

Country

I CAN'T COUNT THE number of times I've been ready to go on a trip, and, at the last minute, spent my time looking frantically for a tag to put on my luggage. Make a set of these great tags for every piece of your luggage; you'll be ready for any trip, whether you travel by air, by land or by sea. Finished size: 3⅛" x 3⅞".

YOU WILL NEED

FABRIC

- Scrap green 1 coordinating print, at least 4" square (tag)
- Scrap green 2 coordinating print, at least 4" square (tag)
- Scrap gold coordinating print, at least 4" square (tag)
- Scrap burgundy coordinating print, at least 4" square (tag)
- ⅓ yd. black print (binding)

NOTIONS

- 1 clear page protector
- 5" square piece of 100 percent cotton batting
- All-purpose threads to match fabrics
- Card stock in the color of your choice
- Copy paper
- Quilt basting spray

TOOLS

- Basic sewing supplies
- Rotary cutting tools
- Presser feet: ¼" foot, walking foot

Instructions
Please read all of the instructions before beginning this project. Refer to Chapter 1: Getting Started for detailed information on tools and techniques. All seams are ¼" wide; use a ¼" foot for accurate seams.

Cut the Materials

FROM	CUT	FOR
Black print	1 strip, 1¼" x 12"	Handle
	1 strip, 2¼" x 22"	Bias binding
Burgundy print	1 square, 4" x 4"	Tag front and back
Gold print	1 square, 4" x 4"	Tag front and back
Green print 1	1 square, 4" x 4"	Tag front and back
Green print 2	1 square, 4" x 4"	Tag front and back
Clear page protector	1 rectangle, 3" x 3¾"*	Tag window
Batting	1 square, 4" x 4"	Tag back

Note: You may need to cut this slightly smaller to fit this into the tag.

Quilt the Luggage Tag Back

1. Lay one 4" x 4" print square face down. Spray both sides of the 4" x 4" batting square, and lay it on top of the first square. Lay another 4" x 4" print square on top of the batting, face up.

2. Quilt the layers as desired. This tag was quilted with a 1" crisscross design.

3. Trim the quilted layers to 3" x 3¾".

Make the Front

1. In the center of the wrong side of another 4" x 4" fabric piece, mark a 1¾" x 2⅛" rectangle.

2. Sew on the marked square, right sides together, to the remaining 4" x 4" fabric piece around all four sides of the drawn rectangle.

3. Cut an X in the center of the sewn rectangle as shown. Be sure to cut as close to the sewn corners as you can, which will make it easier for turning.

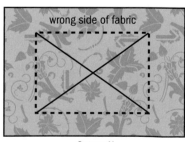

wrong side of fabric

Cut an X.

4. Turn the piece right side out to make a window. Press.

5. Pin the edges together, and baste around all four sides.

6. Topstitch close to the edge of the window.

7. Trim the piece to 3" x 3¾".

Bind the Tag Top Edges

1 Sew binding to one 3" side on both the front and back tag pieces as shown. See Getting Started for details.

Sew the binding.

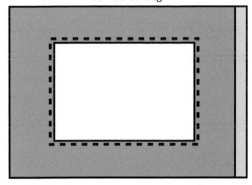

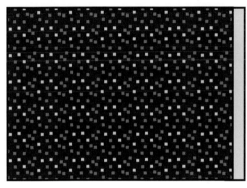

Make the Handle

1 Press ¼" under on both 12" edges of the 1¼" x 12" black strip.

2 Press the strip in half again lengthwise.

3 Fold the pressed strip in half crosswise, matching the raw ends. Baste the ends. Apply anti-fray solution to the ends to secure the threads. Let it dry.

4 Sew the handle to the inside center of the front tag piece, as shown.

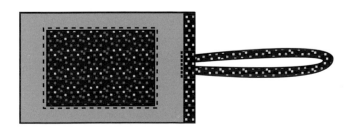

Sew the Tag Together

1 Position the 3" x 3¾" clear page protector on top of the back rectangle piece. Pin the front, wrong sides together, to the back piece to hold together. Trim any excess page protector away.

2 Sew the front and back tag pieces together on three of the sides as shown. Leave the edges with the handle open.

3 Add binding to the three remaining sides. Fold the ¼" overhang under, and fold the binding to the back side. Stitch in the ditch to secure the binding.

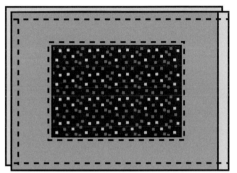

Sew the tag together, and add the binding.

AUBREY'S Tote

THIS LITTLE TOTE was made to match The Messenger Bag. It's a great organizer bag for all of those "little" things that you need to take with you. If you make The Messenger Bag, you will have enough fabric scraps left to create Aubrey's Tote. If you don't, refer to the fabric amounts listed. This bag is a favorite of mine; I've been making this little tote since I was a teenager to keep all of my things together, such as pens, makeup and sewing supplies. This tote works great to help organize your home, too; it's a sure-fire way to keep track of all of those loose game pieces you find. Finished size: 6½" x 8".

YOU WILL NEED

FABRIC

- ⅛ yd. burgundy coordinating print (block)
- ⅛ yd. black coordinating print (block)
- ⅛ yd. gold coordinating print (block)
- ⅛ yd. green 1 coordinating print (tote back, backing/lining)
- ⅓ yd. green 2 coordinating print (block)

NOTIONS

- ⅓ yd. 100 percent cotton batting
- 12" black zipper
- All-purpose threads to match fabrics
- Invisible thread
- Temporary quilt basting spray

TOOLS

- Basic sewing supplies
- Rotary cutting supplies
- Presser feet: ¼" foot, zipper foot, darning foot

Instructions
Please read all of the instructions before beginning this project. Refer to Chapter 1: Getting Started for detailed information on tools and techniques. All seams are ¼" wide; use a ¼" foot for accurate seams.

Cut the Materials

FROM	CUT	FOR
Burgundy print	1 strip, 2⅜" x 7¾"	Block
	1 strip, 1¼" x 10"	Zipper pull
Green 1 print	3 rectangles, 10" x 12"	Tote back, backing/lining
Green 2 print	1 strip, 2⅜" x 7¾"	Block
Gold print	1 strip, 2⅜" x 7¾"	Block
Black print	2 strips, 2⅜" x 7¾"	Block
Batting	2 rectangles, 10" x 12"	Tote front and back

Make the Block

1. Arrange the black, burgundy, green 2 and gold 2⅜" x 7¾" strips in this order: black, burgundy, gold, green 2 and black.

2. Sew the strips, right sides together, along the 7¾" sides. Press the seams in one direction.

Quilt the Block and Tote Back

1 Lay one 10" x 12" green 1 rectangle face down. Spray one 10" x 12" batting rectangle on both sides with quilt basting spray, and lay it on top of the green 1 rectangle. Lay the tote block face up on the batting.

2 Use the darning foot to quilt the layers with a loopy design. See Getting Started for details.

3 Repeat Steps 1 and 2 to layer and quilt the two remaining 10" x 12" green 1 rectangles.

4 Cut both quilted pieces to measure 7¾" x 9½".

Add the Zipper

1 Use the zipper foot to sew the zipper to the front tote block, right sides together, along the 9½" side. Backstitch at the beginning and the end. See Getting Started for details.

2 Open the zipper to make it easier to turn the tote right side out later.

• • • • •

Sew the Tote Bag Together

1 With right sides together, sew the front and back pieces of the tote together around three sides. Backstitch at the beginning and end.

2 Zigzag the raw edges.

3 With the tote bag inside out, line up the side seam with the bottom seam at the corners. Check inside the tote to ensure that the seams match up, then pin the seams in place. Create the purse corners. See Getting Started for details.

4 Sew 1" from the tip of the tote corner.

5 Turn the tote right side out.

Make the Zipper Pull

1 Press under ¼" on each 12¼" edge of the 1¼" x 10" burgundy strip.

2 Fold the strip in half again as shown. Use matching thread to sew the strip along the folded edges.

Fold the strip.

3 Topstitch along the other folded edge.

Stitch the strip.

4 Apply anti-fray solution to the ends of the strip. Let it dry.

5 Thread the strip through the hole in the zipper pull; tie it securely.

RIKKI'S *B*AG

LOVE THE BRIGHT pink and summer brown colors that were used to create this handy square bag. This bag will hold a lot of makeup! (I personally use only one bag, but, my sister used two this size.) This project is a little more challenging than most of the projects in this book, but only because of its different shape, the piping and the way it is stitched together with a curved zipper. But if you read through all of the instructions and follow them carefully, you'll find success! Finished size: 5½" x 8" x 5".

YOU WILL NEED

FABRIC

- [ ] 1 fat quarter light brown (tote sides)
- [ ] 1 fat quarter light pink (tote sides)
- [ ] 1 fat quarter brown, pink and green stripe (tote top and bottom)
- [ ] 1 fat quarter green and cream coordinating print (backing/lining)

NOTIONS

- [ ] 22" light pink or cream zipper
- [ ] Invisible thread
- [ ] ½ yd. 100 percent cotton batting
- [ ] All-purpose threads to match fabrics
- [ ] 1 package light-pink piping
- [ ] Quilt basting spray

TOOLS

- [ ] Basic sewing supplies
- [ ] Rotary cutting supplies
- [ ] Presser feet: ¼" foot, darning foot, zipper foot

PATTERNS

- [ ] Rikki's Bag Top/Side Panel/Bottom Pattern (inside pattern insert)

Instructions Please read all of the instructions before beginning this project. Refer to Chapter 1: Getting Started for detailed information on tools and techniques. All seams are ¼" wide; use a ¼" foot for accurate seams.

Cut the Materials

FROM	CUT	FOR
Light brown print	1 strip, 3½" x 11"	Side panel
Light pink print	1 strip, 3½" x 11"	Side panel
	2 strips, 1½" x 9½"	Strap
	1 strip, 1" x 5"	Zipper pull
Brown, pink and green stripe	1 strip, 3½" x 11"	Side panel
	1 top/bottom panel piece using the top/bottom panel pattern	Top/bottom panel
Green and cream print	1 strip, 5½" x 18½"	Side panel backing/lining
	1 top/bottom panel lining using the top/bottom panel pattern	Top/bottom panel lining
Batting	1 rectangle, 5½" x 18½"	Side panel
	1 top/bottom panel using the top/bottom panel pattern	Top/bottom panel
	1 strip, 1½" x 9½"	Handle

Make the Side Panel

1. With right sides together, sew the 3½" x 11" strips (brown, light pink and brown/pink/green stripe) together along the 11" side. Press the seams in one direction.

2. Cut the above piece into two 5½" x 9¼" pieces as shown. With right sides together, sew the two 5½" x 9¼" pieces along the 5¼" side as shown. Press in the same direction as the other seams.

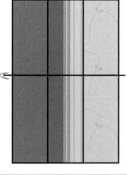

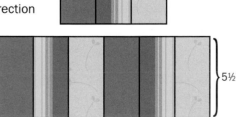

5½"

Quilt the Side Panel

1. Lay the 5½" x 18½" green and cream strip face down. Spray both sides of the 5½" x 18½" batting rectangle, and place it on top of the green and cream strip. Place the side panel face up on top of the batting,

2. Use invisible thread to quilt the layers in a loopy pattern. See Getting Started for details.

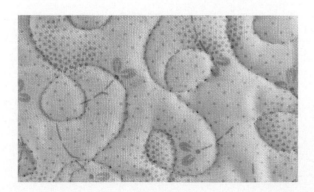

Add the Zipper

1 Use the zipper foot to sew the zipper to the top edge of the quilted side panel, right sides together. Zigzag the raw edges.

2 Topstitch close to the zipper.

3 Use matching thread and the zipper foot to sew the piping to the bottom of the side panel. Match the raw edges of the piping to the raw edge of the side panel as shown.

4 Sew another piece of piping to the top edge of the zipper as shown.

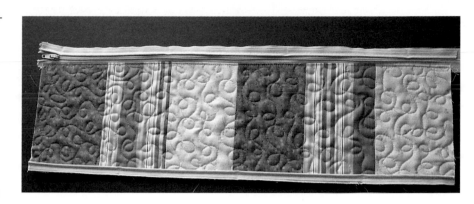

Make the Top and Bottom Panel

1 Lay the green and cream print top/bottom panel lining piece face down. Spray both sides of the batting, cut in the same shape, on top of the green and cream print. Place the brown/pink/green stripe top/bottom panel piece face up on the batting. Line up the pieces carefully, as they need to stay in the exact position for quilting. Pin edges if necessary.

2 Use a loopy design to quilt the layers carefully.

Make the Strap

1 Sew the light pink piping along both 9½" edges of the 1½" x 9½" light pink strap piece as shown.

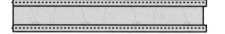

2 Position the two light pink strap pieces, right sides together. Place the batting strip on top of one of the strap pieces. Sew the piece along both seams of the piping.

3 Turn the strap right side out. Press.

4 Topstitch along the edge of the fabric, next to the piping as shown.

5 Sew the strap approximately 2¾" from the edge of the top/bottom quilted piece as shown.

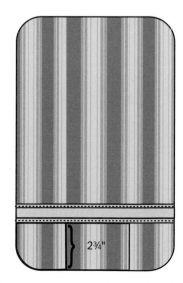

2¾"

Sew the Tote Together

1 Fold the strip in half to find the center of the rectangle zipper piece. Mark the center with pins. Find the center edges of the curved piece as shown below.

2 Unzip the zipper, so that you can turn the bag right side out later.

3 Match the pins on the side panel and the top/bottom piece; place the right sides of the pieces together as shown.

4 Pin the side panel to the top/bottom piece. It will look a little funny, but keep pinning. Pin the unzipped zipper to the top/bottom piece, too.

5 Sew across the zipper part first, and backstitch at each end. Zigzag the raw edges.

6 Sew around the bag. As needed, trim at the corners as shown to make it easier to turn. Zigzag the raw edges.

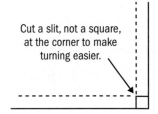

Cut a slit, not a square, at the corner to make turning easier.

Make the Zipper Pull

1 Press ¼" under on both of the 5" sides of the 1" x 5" light pink strip.

2 Press the strip in half, lengthwise.

3 Sew down the folded edge on both sides.

4 Cut an angle at the tip of the strip, and thread that end through the zipper hole. Cut the end straight after it is through the zipper.

5 Tie both ends of the strip together in a knot. Apply anti-fray solution to the ends of the zipper pull. Let it dry.

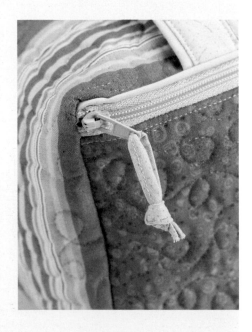

CHAPTER 4

Dressy Bags

LEXI'S BAG

THIS IS ONE of those bags that will make a statement that says, "I have style!" The color alone is regal, and the flowers soften the sharp angles of the bag. The lamp work beads on the zipper pull add an additional charm to this lovely bag. This is my 21-year-old daughter's favorite bag in the book. Who knows? She may end up with it when I'm done with it! We'll just have see, huh, Erin? Finished size: 6" x 16".

YOU WILL NEED

FABRIC

- ⅓ yd. eggplant jacquard fabric (bag)
- ⅓ yd. coordinating print (backing/lining)

NOTIONS

- ⅓ yd. 100 percent cotton batting
- 22" royal plum zipper
- Multicolored quilting thread
- 1 package green miniature lamp work beads
- Fabric glue
- Tape

- 2 yd. cotton cording, ½" diameter (handles)
- All-purpose threads to match fabrics
- ⅓ yd. silk flower trim
- 1 beading eye pin
- Temporary spray adhesive

TOOLS

- Basic sewlng supplies
- Rotary cutting supplies
- Presser feet: ¼" foot, darning foot, zipper foot
- Stiletto
- 3-in-1 beading tool

Instructions
Please read all of the instructions before beginning this project. Refer to Chapter 1: Getting Started for detailed information on tools and techniques. All seams are ¼" wide; use a ¼" foot for accurate seams.

Cut the Materials

FROM	CUT	FOR
Eggplant jacquard	2 rectangles, 9" x 18"	Bag
	2 strips, 2¼" x 30"	Handles
	4 squares, 2¼" x 2¼"	Handles
Coordinating print	2 rectangles, 9" x 18"	Backing/lining
Batting	2 rectangles, 9" x 18"	Bag

Quilt the Bag

1. Lay the 9" x 18" eggplant rectangle face down. Spray both sides of the 9" x 18" batting rectangle, and lay it on top of the eggplant rectangle. Place the 9" x 18" coordinating print right side up on top of the batting.

2. Using the multicolored quilting thread, quilt the layers with a loopy design. See Getting Started for details.

3. Trim the quilted layers to 8½" x 17".

Add the Zipper

1. Use the zipper foot to sew the 22" royal plum zipper to the 17" top edge of the bag. See Getting Started for details.

Sew the Bag Together

1 Unzip the zipper so you can turn the bag right side out later.

2 Sew around the three sides of the purse. Zigzag over the raw edges. Backstitch at the beginning and the end of the seam.

3 With the bag inside out, line up the side seam with the bottom seam at the corners. Check inside the tote to ensure that the seams match up, then pin the seams in place. Create the purse corners 2" from each inside tip, which will make a base for the bag. See Getting Started for details.

Make the Handles

1 Cut two 30" lengths of cording; wrap a piece of tape at the ends of the cording to keep it from splitting.

2 Sew one 2¼" purple square, right sides to-gether, to each end of the 2¼" x 30" purple strips as shown; this will form small pockets. Backstitch at the ends. Trim the corners, and turn right side out.

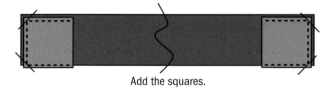

Add the squares.

3 Press under ¼" on both sides of the 30" strips.

4 Tuck the cording inside each small end pocket; insert the cording ¼" to ½" into the pocket.

5 Fold the strip over the cording, and pin it with straight pins along the folds. Use a zipper foot to sew close to the edges of the folds as shown. Use a stiletto or the tip of your seam ripper to hold the fabric together while it goes through the sewing machine. This step is a little tricky, so take your time. Begin and stop sewing approximately 1¼" from both ends of each strap. Backstitch at each end.

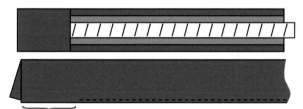

Leave open on both ends.

6 Position and pin the straps to the bag, 2½" from the top edge of the bag, and 3¾" from the sides of the bag.

7 Sew along three sides of the handle tab as shown. Backstitch at the beginning and the end.

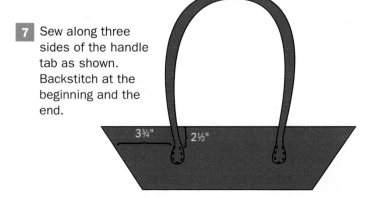

3¾"   2½"

• • • • •
Add the Flower Trim

1 Run a straight line of fabric glue 1½" below the top edge and center of the purse front.

2 Carefully finger press the trim over the glue strip to attach it to the bag. Lay the bag flat to dry.

• • • • •
Make the Zipper Pull

1 String four glass lamp work beads onto an eye pin.

2 Use the 3-in-1 tool to cut off enough of the eye pin; leave ¼" of wire.

3 Use the rounded tip of the 3-in-1 tool to loop the ¼" eye pin wire around the zipper.

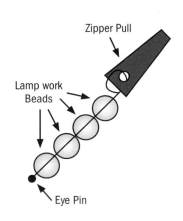

Zipper Pull

Lamp work
Beads

Eye Pin

The APRIL BAG

THIS VERY ARTSY bag features hand-dyed fabric and a checkerboard quilting pattern. The gold chain-link strap is from the hardware store. If you like, change the strap and use different materials, such as decorator cording for curtains. The furry trim at the bottom of the purse is a fun trim; it is optional, depending on your taste. After I made this purse, I realized that I really like green and purple together, and I remembered a robe that I had made — and loved — in the same combination more than 20 years ago. Make this purse with your favorite combinations of colors. Make several; it's so easy! Finished size: 6½" x 13¾".

YOU WILL NEED

FABRIC

- [ ] 1 fat quarter purple and green hand-dyed fabric (purse front)
- [ ] ⅓ yd. coordinating purple print 1 (lining, lining pocket)
- [ ] ⅓ yd. coordinating purple print 2 (purse back)
- [ ] 1 fat quarter green print (purse front)
- [ ] ⅓ yd. muslin (backing)

NOTIONS

- [ ] ⅓ yd. 100 percent cotton batting
- [ ] 14" royal plum zipper
- [ ] 45" gold chain, ⅜" wide
- [ ] 1 package assorted salwag beads
- [ ] 1 package furry fiber trim (optional)
- [ ] ¼ yd. woven, iron-on interfacing

- [ ] All-purpose threads to match fabrics
- [ ] ⁷⁄₁₆" extra-large eyelets
- [ ] 1 beading eye pin
- [ ] Temporary spray adhesive
- [ ] Clear tape

TOOLS

- [ ] Basic sewing supplies
- [ ] Rotary cutting supplies
- [ ] Hammer
- [ ] Presser feet: ¼" foot, walking foot with guide, zipper foot

- [ ] 2 pairs of micro-tip pliers
- [ ] ⁷⁄₁₆" eyelet tool
- [ ] 3-in-1 beading tool

Instructions
Please read all of the instructions before beginning this project. Refer to Chapter 1: Getting Started for detailed information on tools and techniques. All seams are ¼" wide; use a ¼" foot for accurate seams.

Cut the Materials

FROM	CUT	FOR
Purple and green hand-dyed print	1 rectangle, 6" x 9½"	Purse front
Purple print 1	2 rectangles, 8" x 14½"	Lining
	2 rectangles, 5" x 7½"	Lining pocket
Purple print 2	1 rectangle, 9½" x 14½"	Purse back
Green print	1 rectangle, 9½" x 10"	Purse front
Muslin	2 rectangles, 9½" x 14½"	Front and back backing
Batting	2 rectangles, 9½" x 14½"	Purse front and back
Woven iron-on interfacing	1 rectangle, 5" x 7½"	Lining pocket

Make the Purse Front

1 With right sides together, sew the 6" x 9½" purple and green rectangle and the 9½" x 10" green rectangle together along the 9½" side as shown. Press the seams open.

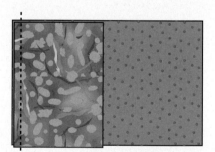

Sew the rectangles together.

2 Lay one 9½" x 14½" muslin rectangle face down. Spray both sides of the 9½" x 14½" batting rectangle with quilt basting spray, and place it on top of the muslin rectangle. Place the purse front face up on top of the batting.

3 Quilt the layers as shown; use a crisscross design, and space the lines ¼" apart. See Getting Started for details.

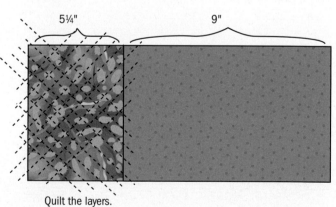

5¼"　　9"

Quilt the layers.

4 Trim the quilted purse front to 8" x 14½"; cut the piece so the purple section measures 5¼" wide and the green section measures 9" wide.

5 Zigzag a row of fur trim at the bottom of the purse front; turn the bag after each row is stitched to achieve six rows of fur trim and a "thicker" look. Use matching thread in the needle and the bobbin.

6 Place a piece of clear tape over the fur as shown; this will keep it away from the seam line.

Make the Purse Back

1 Lay the remaining 9½" x 14½" muslin rectangle face down. Spray both sides of a 9½" x 14½" batting rectangle with quilt basting spray, and lay it on top of the muslin rectangle. Lay the 9½" x 14½" purple purse back face up on top of the batting.

2 Quilt the purse back layers in crisscross design, and space the lines ¼" apart. See Getting Started for details.

Add the Zipper

1 Use the zipper foot to sew the 14" royal plum zipper onto the purse front and back. See Getting Started for details.

Sew the Purse Together

1 Unzip the zipper; this will make it easier to turn the purse right side out.

2 With right sides together, sew the three sides of the purse together as shown. Zigzag the raw edges. Turn the purse right side out.

Unzip zipper before sewing.

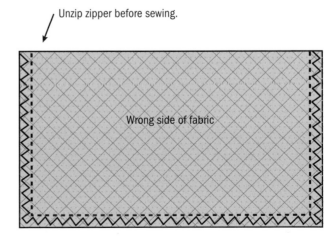

Wrong side of fabric

Tip

Can't find what you need at the fabric store?

Consider going a different route. I looked a lot of places to find the perfect chain for the strap on this purse. I finally found it at the hardware store! This chain link was available in silver, gold and black; the gold and black felt the best in my hand, and the gold matched the eyelets perfectly. I admit it: The hardware store is my second-favorite store, next to the fabric store!

Make the Purse Pocket

1 Iron a 5" x 7½" piece of woven, iron-on interfacing to the wrong side of one of the 5" x 7½" purple print 1 rectangles.

2 With right sides together, sew the remaining 5" x 7½" rectangle to the interfaced rectangle on all four sides; leave a 3" opening to turn the piece right side out, as shown. Clip the corners.

3 Turn the pocket right side out. Press.

4 Topstitch two rows that are ¼" apart across the open end of the pocket.

5 Center the pocket on one of the 8" x 14½" purple rectangles; position the pocket 2" from the top of the rectangle as shown.

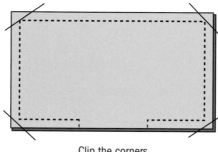

Clip the corners.

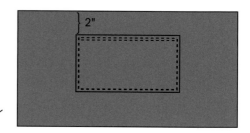

Add the pocket.

Sew the Purse Lining Together

1 With right sides together, sew the two 8" x 14½" purple print 1 rectangles together on both 8" sides and the bottom edge; be sure to position the rectangles so the pocket opening is facing up. Backstitch at each end of stitching.

2 Without turning the lining right side out, press ¼" of the top edge to the wrong side. Keep this wrong side out.

3 Position the lining inside the purse.

4 Pin the pressed edge of the lining to the lower side of the zipper, beneath the teeth.

5 Hand stitch the lining to the zipper.

Add the Large Eyelets and Strap

1. Position the eyelets close to the sides of the purse, just below the zipper. Make sure there are no seams to get in the way of the eyelet.

2. Draw a pencil circle inside of the eyelet hole.

3. Use sharp scissors to carefully cut out the marked circle. Avoid removing too much fabric; the fabric needs to stretch around the eyelet to hold it securely.

4. Follow the manufacturer's directions to attach the eyelet.

5. Repeat Steps 1 through 4 for the other eyelet.

6. Use the micro tip pliers to open the end of the chain link. The link is a lot tougher than you would think. It took a little muscle to get these open.

7. Thread the chain through the eyelet.

8. Close the opened loop around the ninth loop from the end as shown.

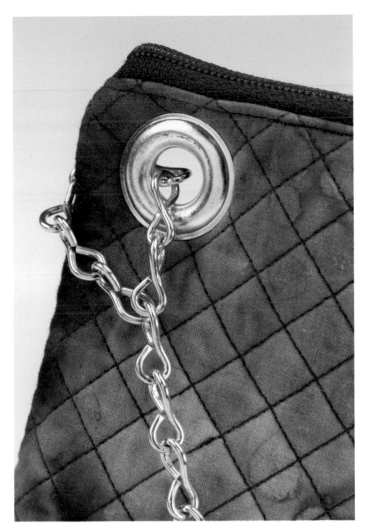

Tip

When using this size of eyelet, I have found that using a scrap piece of marble or using cement underneath the purse while you hit the tool with the hammer will ensure a better eyelet connection. My counter top with a protective surface was not hard enough.

Make the Beaded Zipper Pull

1. Choose three different shapes and colors of beads.

2. Thread the beads onto the eye pin. Use the 3-in-1 tool to cut off enough of the eye pin; leave ¼" of wire.

3. Use the rounded tip of the 3-in-1 tool to loop the ¼" eye pin wire around the zipper.

ALLIE'S PURSE

I WAS LOOKING FOR unique trims and handles for the bags in this book when I ran across these bobbins at the Antique Textiles booth at a show. When I saw them, I knew that they would be perfect handles. The design for this purse came very easily after that. If you can't find antique bobbins, use two 10"-long dowels that are 1" in diameter. I also used antique buttons. If you don't have antique buttons, buy some that look good together; just make sure they all look different to add interest to the piece. I found the trim through Nifty Thrifty Dry Goods. This supplier has a lot of antique trims; describe the trim or lace, and she will match it. See Contributors and Resources for more details about the bobbin and trim suppliers. Finished size: 8½" x 15" x 3" (excluding handles).

YOU WILL NEED

FABRIC

- ⅓ yd. green large-floral print
  (block, side panels, back)

- ⅓ yd. medium-green coordinating print
  (block, lining, lining pocket)

- ⅛ yd. dark-green coordinating print (block)

- ⅛ yd. burgundy coordinating print (block)

- ⅛ yd. purple coordinating print (block)

- ⅓ yd. black coordinating print (binding, straps)

- ⅓ yd. muslin (backing)

NOTIONS

- 1 yd. trim to match fabrics, ½" wide

- 1 cream or black zipper, 7" long

- All-purpose threads to match fabrics

- 3 black buttons, 1⅛" to 1¼" in diameter

- 1 black button, 1" in diameter

- ½ yd. 100 percent cotton batting

- ¼ yd. woven, iron-on interfacing

- ⅛ yd. stiff, fusible interfacing

- Craft adhesive

- Anti-fray solution

- 2 polka-dot bobbins, each 10" long, or 2 wooden dowels, each 1" x 10", and paintbrush and paint to embellish dowels as desired

TOOLS

- Basic sewing supplies

- Rotary cutting supplies

- Presser feet: ¼" foot, walking foot, zipper foot

Instructions
Please read all of the instructions before beginning this project. Refer to Chapter 1: Getting Started for detailed information on tools and techniques. All seams are ¼" wide; use a ¼" foot for accurate seams.

Cut the Materials

FROM	CUT	FOR
Green large-floral print	1 rectangle, 6½" x 8¼"	Block
	1 strip, 3¼" x 30"	Side panel
	1 rectangle, 8¼" x 15"	Back panel
Medium-green print	1 strip, 4½" x 8¼"	Block
	2 rectangles, 8¼" x 14¾"	Lining
	1 strip, 3¼" x 30"	Side panel lining
	2 rectangles, 6" x 8¼"	Lining pocket
	2 rectangles, 2¾" x 13"	Purse base insert
Dark-green print	1 strip, 2" x 8¼"	Block
Burgundy print	1 strip, 2" x 8¼"	Block
Purple print	1 strip, 2" x 8¼"	Block
Black print	1 strip, 3½" x 44"	Handle straps
	1 strip, 2¼" x 7¼"	Purse closure
	Bias strips as needed, 2¼" wide	Binding
Muslin	2 rectangles, 8¼" x 15"	Front and back backing
	1 strip, 3¼" x 30"	Side panel backing
Batting	2 rectangles, 8¼" x 15"	Front and back panel
	1 strip, 3¼" x 30"	Side panel
	1 strip, 1½" x 44"	Straps
	1 strip, ¾" x 7"	Purse closure
Stiff, fusible interfacing	1 strip, 2¾" x 13"	Purse base insert
Woven, iron-on interfacing	1 rectangle, 6" x 8¼"	Lining pocket

Make the Front Panel Block

1 With right sides together, sew the 2" x 8¼" dark green, burgundy and purple strips together as shown. Press in one direction.

2 Sew the 6½" x 8¼" green large-floral rectangle to the right of the block. Press.

3 Sew the 4½" x 8¼" medium-green print rectangle to the right of the block. Press.

Sew the strips together.

Quilt the Front, Side and Back Panels

1 Lay one 8¼" x 15" muslin rectangle face down. Spray both sides of an 8¼" x 15" batting rectangle with quilt basting spray, and lay it on top of the muslin. Place the pieced front face up on top of the batting.

2 Lay one 8¼" x 15" muslin rectangle face down. Spray both sides of an 8¼" x 15" batting rectangle with quilt basting spray, and lay it on top of the muslin. Place the 8¼" x 15" green large-floral back face up on top of the batting.

3 Lay the 3¼" x 30" muslin rectangle face down. Spray both sides of the 3¼" x 30" batting strip with quilt basting spray, and lay it on top of the muslin. Place the 3¼" x 30" green large-floral side strip face up on top of the batting.

4 Use a 1½"-wide checkerboard pattern to quilt the front, side panels and back as shown. Measure the distance between the strips on the left side of the front panel, and use that as the stitching distance.

5 Trim the pieces to straighten the edges; make sure the front and back panels are the same size.

Add the Trim and Buttons

1 Sew a 9" piece of trim down the center of the medium-green print section on the purse front panel. Make sure there is an extra ¼" on the right edge of the medium-green print for the seam allowance. If this isn't planned, the trim will be off center when the purse is finished.

2 Sew the three large buttons onto the trim as shown.

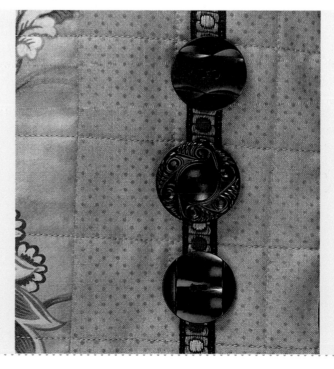

• • • • •
Make the Lining Pocket

1 Cut a 6" x 8¼" piece of woven, iron-on interfacing.

2 Press the interfacing to the wrong side of one of the 6" x 8¼" medium-green pocket pieces.

3 Sew the two pocket pieces right sides together; leave an opening for turning. Turn the pocket right side out, and press.

4 Use the zipper foot to sew the open side of the pocket to the 7" cream zipper. See Getting Started for details.

5 Pin the pocket to one of the 8¼" x 14¾" medium-green lining pieces. Position the pocket up-side down, 1½" from the top edge and 3¼" from each side edge.

6 Fold the zipper ends in toward the underside of the zipper, so only the metal ends of the zipper are exposed as shown. Backstitch at each end.

7 Turn the pocket down to sew it to the lining. Sew close to the edge around the three sides.

8 Tuck ¼" under each end of a 6" piece of trim. Use matching thread to sew the trim along both edges. Sew to the right side of the pocket. Note: You will be covering the edge of the pocket and the zipper edges; if desired, you can sew another piece of trim on the other side.

• • • • •
Sew the Purse Together

1 Pin the 8¼" x 15" front lining piece, wrong sides together, to the quilted front panel. Sew close to the edges.

2 Pin the side panel lining, wrong sides together, to the quilted side panel. Sew close to the edges.

3 Pin the "pocket" back lining piece, wrong sides together, to the quilted back. Sew close to the edges.

4 Pin and sew the front panel, wrong sides together, to the side panel. Clip the side panel at the corners for easy sewing. It may sound wrong to sew with wrong sides together; in order for the binding to show, this is the correct way.

5 Repeat Step 4 to add the purse back as shown.

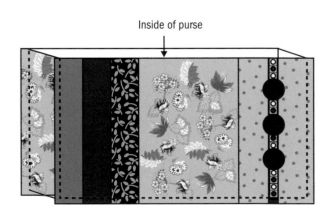

Inside of purse

Add the Binding

1 Sew enough 2¼"-wide black print bias strips together to measure around the three sides of the purse. See Getting Started for details.

2 Sew the binding on all three sides of the front and back of the purse.

3 Sew enough 2¼"-wide black print bias strips together to measure around the three sides of the front and back of the purse.

4 Sew the binding around the top edge. Tuck the side binding pieces toward the side panels.

Tip

For the handles on this bag, I used one green bobbin with beige dots and one beige bobbin with green dots. The supplier can't guarantee the colors, so ask for what is available, and choose fabric colors to coordinate with the bobbins, like I did. Or, create your own set of custom handles with two dowels that you paint to coordinate with the fabrics.

Make the Straps

1 Press under ¼" on the 44" side of the 3½" x 44" black print strip.

2 Spray quilt basting spray to one side of the 1½" x 44" batting piece, and center it on the wrong side of the black print strip. Sew down the center and both side edges of the strap. Cut the strip into four 9" strips to make four handle straps. See Getting Started for details.

3 Apply anti-fray solution to each end of each 9" strip.

4 Position one strap ¾" from each end of a polka dot bobbin. Apply glue to the center of the strap to secure it to the bobbin; lay the unit flat to dry, as shown. Repeat for the other bobbin handle.

5 When the straps are dry, match the ends up and baste together.

6 Position the straps approximately 3" from the sides of the purse. Sew the straps to the inside of the purse, and stitch in the ditch.

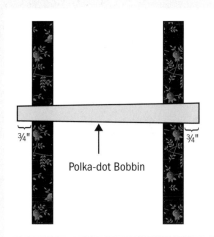

¾"   ¾"

Polka-dot Bobbin

Make the Purse Closure

1 Cut a 2¾" piece of trim. Fold under ¼" on each end of the trim. Apply anti-fray solution to each end of the trim.

2 Position and pin the trim so it is in the center of the front of the purse and 1¾" from the top of the purse. Sew the trim in place on each side, on top of the folded edges. Backstitch to make sure the trim is secure.

3 Press ¼" under the two short sides of the 2¼" x 7¼" black closure strip, then press ¼" under on the two long sides of the strip. Press the strip again, in half lengthwise.

4 Tuck the batting piece inside the folded black print strip. Sew around the edges on all four sides.

5 Sew the 1" black button to the end of the closure.

6 Sew the closure to the inside back of the purse. Position it between the handles; make sure that the closure is positioned to fit within the trim loop. Stitch in the ditch of the binding as shown.

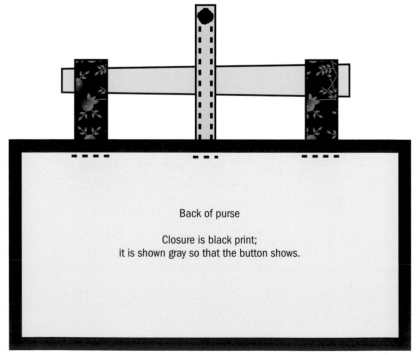

Back of purse

Closure is black print;
it is shown gray so that the button shows.

Make the Purse Base Insert

1 Cover the 2¾" x 13" stiff, fusible interfacing with the two 2¾" x 13" medium-green rectangles, right sides out. Iron the fabric on each side to fuse it.

2 Zigzag around all four edges of the rectangle. Place the insert at the bottom of the purse for stability.

DANIELLE'S Purse

THIS LITTLE PURSE is perfect for any time you want a small purse for just the incidentals. It can be made to be very dressy with velvets and silks, or made to be very casual with corduroy fabrics or denim. Change the tassel, or use a decorative button, a large and beautiful bead or a pretty shell. Use your imagination with the fabrics, embellishments and handles, and this bag will always look wonderful. Finished size: 8" x 10".

YOU WILL NEED

FABRIC

- ⅓ yd. pink decorator print (purse back/flap)
- ⅓ yd. sage coordinating solid (purse front, lining, tabs)

NOTIONS

- ⅓ yd. 100 percent cotton batting
- 1 bundle of fibers (tassel)
- Anti-fray solution

- All-purpose threads to match fabrics
- 1 pink rayon drapery cord, 29" long (handle)
- 1 black snap, ½" in diameter

TOOLS

- Basic sewing supplies
- Rotary cutting supplies
- Presser feet: ¼" foot, walking foot, darning foot

PATTERNS

- Danielle Purse Back/Flap Pattern (inside pattern insert)
- Danielle Purse Front Pattern (inside pattern insert)

Instructions Please read all of the instructions before beginning this project. Refer to Chapter 1: Getting Started for detailed information on tools and techniques. All seams are ¼" wide; use a ¼" foot for accurate seams.

Cut the Materials

FROM	CUT	FOR
Pink decorator print	1 purse back/flap (use pattern)	Purse back/flap
Sage solid	1 purse back/flap (use pattern)	Purse back/flap
	2 purse fronts (use pattern)	Purse front
	2 strips, 1¾" x 5"	Handle tabs
Batting	1 purse back/flap (use pattern)	Purse back/flap
	1 purse front (use pattern)	Purse front

Make the Tassel

1 Cut a bundle of fibers that measures 10" long.

2 Knot a 10" piece of fiber at the center of the fibers; leave the ties on the end.

Tie the fibers.

3 Fold the fibers at the knot. Use another piece of fiber to tie the folded bundle into a tassel; position the fiber 1" from the fold.

Create the tassel.

Make the Purse Back/Flap

1 Lay the pink purse back/flap piece face down. Spray one side of the batting purse back/flap with quilt basting spray, and lay it, spray side down, on top of the pink purse back/flap piece. Pin the edges to secure them.

2 Pin the sage purse back/flap right sides together to the pink purse back/flap.

3 Sew from one dot to the other dot as shown. Trim the tip, and clip to the dot to allow you to turn the piece right side out. Press.

4 Baste the lower layers together.

5 Use a loopy design to quilt the layers. See Getting Started for details. Set it aside.

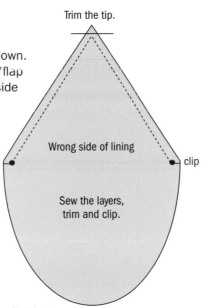

Trim the tip.

Wrong side of lining

clip

Sew the layers, trim and clip.

Make the Purse Front

1 Lay one sage purse front piece right side down. Spray the back side of the batting purse front piece with quilt basting spray, and lay it, spray side down, on top of the sage purse front piece.

2 Quilt the layers in a checkerboard pattern as shown; space the lines ¾" apart.

3 With right sides together, sew the remaining sage purse front to the quilted layers; stitch across the top edge as shown.

4 Open the purse front and press. Topstitch close to the seam, along the lining side, as shown.

5 Turn the lining to the back, and press. Pin the edges together, and baste ⅛" from the raw edge.

6 With right sides together, sew the purse front to the purse back/flap as shown. Zigzag the edges, and turn the piece right side out.

Stitch the layers together.

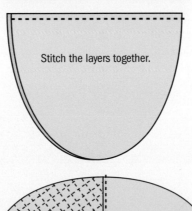

Open the purse, press and topstitch.

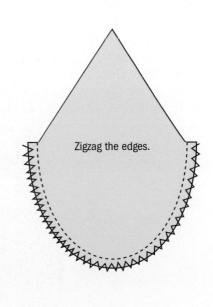

Zigzag the edges.

7 Sew the tassel to the purse flap as shown. Trim the tassel so it is even with the bottom of the bag.

8 With the male and female sides of the snap connected, position the snap on the front of the bag so the snap will be hidden when the flap is closed. Use pins to mark the snap position on the purse front and on the flap.

9 Separate the snaps. Sew the male snap to the purse flap and the female snap to the purse body as shown.

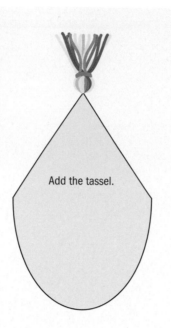

Add the tassel.

Make the Tabs and Handle

1 Press under ⅜" along both 5" edges of each handle tab. Fold the strip in half lengthwise, and press it again.

2 Topstitch down both sides, close to the edge.

3 Thread the tab through the loop on the cording Fold in the tab half, and sew the ends together to make another loop as shown.

4 Sew the tabs with the handle attached to the inside seam on each side of the purse. Apply anti-fray solution to the ends of each tab.

Cording

Tab

Thread the tab.

CHAPTER 5

Sporty Totes

JESSICA'S Backpack

I FELL IN LOVE with the red and black plaid in this backpack design, and I loved the toile fabric, too. When I put the two together, this backpack design came to me. The plaid was a dress from a secondhand store, and the toile was a scrap piece of fabric from a secondhand store. Like they say, someone else's junk becomes someone else's treasure. I really believe that this bag turned out to be a treasure! It looks small, but it holds a lot. It's perfect to tote your books, haul your quilting supplies or take antiquing! This also would make a wonderful child's backpack in his or her favorite colors. Finished size: 11" x 15" x 2".

YOU WILL NEED

FABRIC

- ⅓ yd. black and red plaid (backpack)
- ⅓ yd. black and cream toile (pocket)
- ⅓ yd. black solid (backing/lining)

NOTIONS

- 1 black zipper, 9"
- All-purpose threads to match fabrics
- Invisible thread
- 1 package black twill tape, ½" wide
- ⅓ yd. 100 percent cotton batting
- 1 package black webbing, 1" wide
- 1 package black webbing, ⅜" wide
- 1 plastic side-release buckle, ⅜" wide
- 1 black plastic cord lock with ¼" hole
- ¾ yd. red nylon cording, ¼" diameter
- ³⁄₁₆"-wide fusible tape
- 1 package eyelets, ³⁄₁₆"
- 1 yd. black and cream check ribbon, ⅜" wide
- Transparent tape

TOOLS

- Basic sewing supplies
- Matches or lighter
- Rotary cutting supplies
- 1 punch and set tool, ³⁄₁₆"
- Presser feet: ¼" foot, darning foot, zipper foot

PATTERNS

- Jessica's Backpack Flap Pattern (inside pattern insert)

Instructions
Please read all of the instructions before beginning this project. Refer to Chapter 1: Getting Started for detailed information on tools and techniques. All seams are ¼" wide; use a ¼" foot for accurate seams.

Cut the Materials

FROM	CUT	FOR
Black and red plaid	2 rectangles, 11½" x 17"	Front and back
	1 rectangle, 6" x 7"	Flap
Toile	1 rectangle, 8½" x 9"	Pocket
	2 rectangles, 6½" x 11½"	Upper backing/lining
	1 rectangle, 6" x 7"	Flap lining
	1 strip, 1½" x 3¼"	Loop cover
Black	1 rectangle, 8½" x 9"	Pocket lining
	2 rectangles, 11" x 11½"	Lower backing/lining
	As needed, 2¼"-wide bias strips	Binding
Batting	1 rectangle, 8½" x 9"	Pocket
	2 rectangles, 11½" x 17	Front and back
	1 rectangle, 6" x 7"	Flap

Make the Pocket

1 Lay the 8½" x 9" toile rectangle face down. Spray both sides of the 8½" x 9" batting rectangle with quilt basting spray, and lay it on top of the toile rectangle. Lay the 8½" x 9" black rectangle face up on top of the batting.

2 Quilt the layers together with a loopy design; use a darning foot, invisible thread in the needle and black thread in the bobbin. See Getting Started for details.

3 Trim all the edges straight.

Add the Zipper

1 With right sides together, sew the 9" black zipper on with a zipper foot. Sew the zipper to only one edge of the pocket. See Getting Started for details.

2 Zigzag the raw edge. Topstitch close to the zipper. Set aside.

Quilt the Front and Back

1 With right sides together, sew the 6½" x 11½" upper lining to the 11" x 11½" lower lining pieces along the 11½" side. Press the seams open.

2 Lay the 11½" x 17" front plaid piece face down. Spray both sides of the 11½" x 17" batting rectangle with quilt basting spray; lay it on top of the front plaid piece. Lay the front lining piece face up on top of the batting. Repeat for the back pieces.

3 Quilt the layers together. See Getting Started for details.

4 Trim all of the edges straight. Set the front and back aside.

Make and Quilt the Flap

1 Lay the 6" x 7" plaid rectangle face down. Spray both sides of the 6" x 7" batting rectangle with quilt basting spray, and lay it on top of the plaid rectangle. Place the 6" x 7" toile rectangle face up on top of the batting.

2 With invisible thread in the needle and matching thread in the bobbin, use a darning foot to quilt a loopy design.

3 Use the backpack flap pattern to cut one backpack flap from the quilted layers created in Step 2.

4 Cut enough 2¼"-wide black bias binding to go around the edges of the flap as shown. Zigzag the remaining raw edge. See Getting Started for details. Set the flap aside.

Add the Pocket

1 Position the pocket 1¼" from both the right and left sides, and 1¼" from the base of the front panel. Pin the pocket in place.

2 Sew ⅛" from the edge on all four sides. One side will be the zipper's edge.

3 Sew the ⅜"-wide checkerboard trim on all four sides as shown; miter the corners as you go.

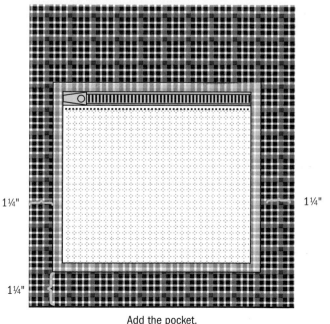

1¼"   1¼"

1¼"

Add the pocket.

• • • • •

Add the Straps

1 Cut a 6¾" length of 1"-wide webbing. Fold the webbing in half lengthwise.

2 Pin the webbing in place 2½" below the top edge and center of the back panel. Make a 1" space between the webbing.

3 Use matching thread to sew the webbing loop, ¼" from the ends, as shown. Backstitch at the beginning and the end.

4 Cut the remaining 1"-wide webbing in half to make two equal lengths for the straps.

5 Position the two pieces, side to side, underneath the handle; they will be touching the tips of the handle as shown.

Add the loop.

2½"

1"

6 Pin the 1½" x 3¼" piece of toile over the raw edges of the webbing; cover all of the ends. Baste along the four edges, ⅛" from the edge.

7 Sew the ⅜"-wide checkerboard trim around the edges of the toile cover, as you did before on the pocket.

8 Pin the two bottom edges of the webbing 1¼" in from the bottom corners. The raw edges of the webbing will match the raw edge of the back panel as shown.

Sew the Front and Back Together

1 With right sides together, pin the backpack front and back panels. Keep the straps away from the seams.

2 Sew the sides and bottom together; zigzag the raw edges. Turn the bag right side out. Press the seams.

3 Make the base of the backpack by sewing the corners approximately 1½" from the tip. Do not sew over the webbing.

Add the Twill Tape to the Top Edge

1 Sew the ½"-wide black twill tape across the top edge of the bag; center the tape over the raw edge.

2 Fold the raw edge under ¼" at the end of the twill tape for a clean finish as shown.

3 Stick the ³⁄₁₆"-wide fusible tape to the underside of the twill tape. Use an iron to quickly press the tape in place and remove the paper backing..

4 Fold the twill tape to the inside of the backpack; press the tape to the underside.

5 Topstitch the twill tape from the outside so that you know where the stitching is going to go.

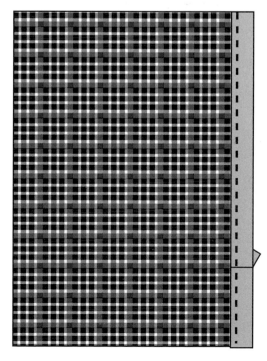

Topstitch the twill tape.

Add the Eyelets

1 Beginning at the side seams, approximately ¼" from the seam, position the eyelets so they are 1" from the top edge and 1¼" apart. Place five eyelets on each side for a total of 10 eyelets; otherwise, the cording will not be in the right place for the bag.

2 Follow the manufacturer's directions for installing the eyelets. Do not make the holes too big; the fabric will stretch over the eyelet.

Add the Flap

1 Pin and sew the flap with the stitch in the ditch method to the inside of the backpack, as shown. Be sure the toile is facing inside the backpack.

Add the Cording

1 Cut the length of red nylon cording in half. Use a match or lighter to quickly burn the ends of the cord. Heat the tips of the cord just long enough to seal the threads together; you don't want the ends to turn black.

2 Wrap a small piece of transparent tape at each end of the cord so that the cord will go through the eyelets easily.

3 Beginning at the two center eyelets, thread the eyelets from the outside to the inside in both directions.

4 Wrap transparent tape around the other two ends of the other length of cord. Thread the cording through the cord lock hole, and remove the tape.

5 Tie a knot at the loose end of each cord as shown.

• • • • •
Add the Side-Release Buckle and Attach the Flap

1 Cut two pieces, each 1½" long, from the ⅜"-wide webbing.

2 Thread one of the pieces through the male half of the ⅜" side-release buckle. Fold the webbing in half, and sew the end pieces together.

3 Attach the buckle to the flap; stitch in the ditch. Apply anti-fray solution to the ends.

4 Thread the other piece of webbing through the female end of the side-release buckle; baste the ends together. Apply anti-fray solution to the ends.

5 Fold the ends of the webbing under, and sew them just above the center pocket as shown.

BRADFORD Duffel

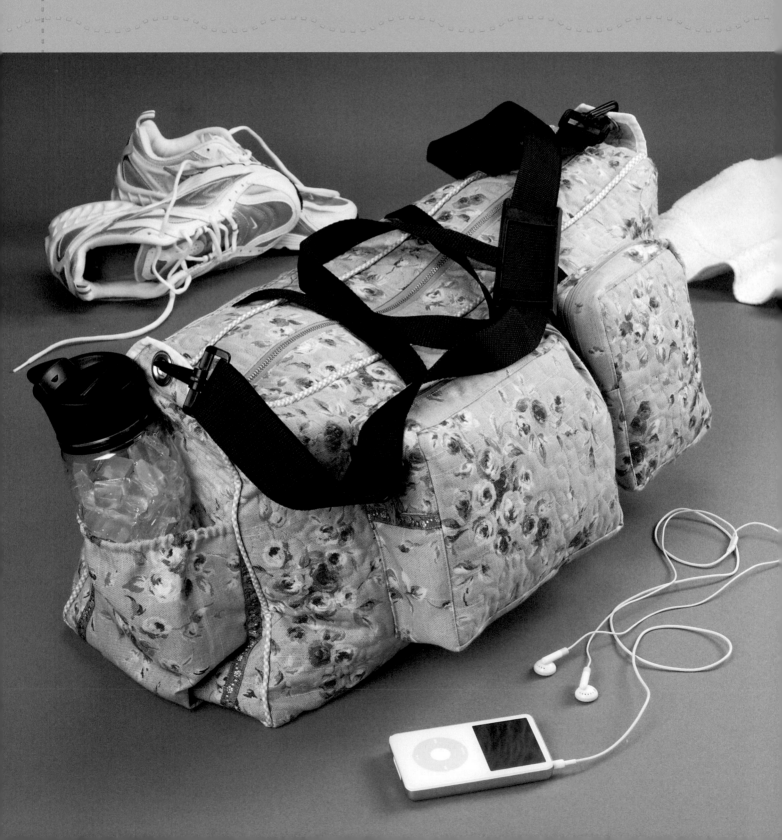

WHO SAYS THAT duffel bags have to be boring? I knew that I wanted to make a duffel bag for this book. When it came time to choose the fabric, I saw this particular floral print and said, "That is the one!" The fabric just felt right, and I think it turned out beautifully. I loved adding the floral trim and checkerboard piping as accents; they both add little touches that keep this duffel bag from being boring. Get creative; put together a bag that has several coordinating prints and trim. The three-dimensional pockets are challenging for a beginner, so if you want, make the flat pocket on both sides. Finished size: 11" x 23" x 8".

YOU WILL NEED

FABRIC

- 1½ yd. floral decorator fabric (bag)
- 1½ yd. green/beige check print fabric (backing/lining)

NOTIONS

- 1 yd. 100 percent cotton batting
- 2 yd. pink floral trim, $3/8$" wide
- 2 rose zippers, each 14"
- 1 metal camel zipper, 24"
- 1 package black webbing, 1" wide
- 2 black plastic swivel hooks, 1½"
- 1 shoulder strap cushion, 1½" wide
- 2 packages bias-corded white piping
- White chalk pencil
- Heavy card stock

- All-purpose threads to match fabrics
- ½ yd. pink/cream checked ribbon, ½" wide
- 1 rose zipper, 12"
- $1/3$ yd. elastic, ¼" wide
- 1½ yd. black webbing, 1½" wide
- 1 black plastic slider, 1½"
- 2 large gold eyelets, $7/16$"
- 1 package green quilt binding
- ¼ yd. stiff, fusible interfacing
- Safety pin

TOOLS

- Basic sewing supplies
- Presser feet: ¼" foot, darning foot, zipper foot
- 1 eyelet tool, $7/16$"

- Rotary cutting tools
- Hammer

PATTERNS

- The Bradford Duffel Bag Should Strap Tab (inside pattern insert)
- The Bradford Duffel Bag Side Panel (inside pattern insert)

Instructions
Please read all of the instructions before beginning this project. Refer to Chapter 1: Getting Started for detailed information on tools and techniques. All seams are ¼" wide; use a ¼" foot for accurate seams.

Cut the Materials

FROM	CUT	FOR
Floral print*	2 rectangles, 24" x 31½"	Front and back
	2 rectangles, 9" x 12"	Side panels
	2 rectangles, 8" x 9"	Side panel pockets
	1 rectangle, 8" x 14"	Large flat pocket
	1 strip, 5" x 24"	Zipper panel
	1 rectangle, 8" x 10"	Large 3-D pocket
	2 strips, 1½" x 14"	Large 3-D pocket
	1 strip, 3⅛" x 17½"	Large 3-D pocket
	1 rectangle, 6" x 8"	Small 3-D pocket
	2 strips, 1½" x 12"	Small 3-D pocket
	1 strip, 3⅛" x 13"	Small 3-D pocket
	4 squares, 5" x 5"	Shoulder strap tabs
Check print	2 rectangles, 24" x 31½"	Front and back backing/lining
	2 rectangles, 9" x 12"	Side panel backing/lining
	2 rectangles, 8" x 9"	Side panel pocket lining
	1 strip, 5" x 24"	Zipper panel lining
	1 rectangle, 8" x 14"	Large flat pocket backing/lining
	1 rectangle 8" x 10"	Large 3-D pocket lining
	2 strips, 1½" x 14"	Large 3-D pocket lining
	1 strip, 3⅛" x 17½"	Large 3-D pocket lining
	1 rectangle, 6" x 8"	Small 3-D pocket backing/lining
	2 strips, 1½" x 12"	Small 3-D pocket lining
	1 strip, 3⅛" x 13"	Small 3-D pocket lining
	2 rectangles, 8" x 13"	Duffel bag base
	As needed, bias strips, 2¼" wide	Binding
Batting	2 rectangles, 9" x 12"	Side panels
	1 rectangle, 5" x 24"	Zipper panel
	2 rectangles, 24" x 31½"	Bag front and back
	1 rectangle, 8" x 14"	Large flat side pocket
	1 rectangle, 8" x 10"	Large 3-D pocket
	1 rectangle, 6" x 8"	Small 3-D pocket
	2 squares, 5" x 5"	Shoulder strap tabs

Note: The zipper strap tabs will be cut later.

Make the Side Panels

1 Lay the 9" x 12" decorator fabric rectangle face down. Spray both sides of one 9" x 12" batting rectangle with quilt basting spray; lay it on top of the decorator fabric. Lay the check lining rectangle on top, face up.

2 Quilt the layers in a loopy design, or as desired. Repeat for the other side panel.

3 Use the Duffel Bag Side Panel Pattern to cut two side panels from the quilted layers.

Make the Side Panel Pockets

1 With right sides together, sew the 8" x 9" decorator rectangle to the 8" x 9" lining fabric across the 9" edge as shown. Press the seam in one direction.

2 Turn the lining fabric to the wrong side of the pocket.

Wrong side of pocket lining

Sew the pocket.

3 Topstitch a casing ⅜" from the top edge as shown.

4 With a safety pin attached to one end of the 5" piece of ¼"-wide elastic, thread the elastic through the casing. When the unpinned end of the elastic reaches the edge of the pocket, secure it in place with several rows of stitching. Secure the other end of the elastic when it reaches the end. Remove the safety pin. Repeat for the other pocket.

Create the casing.

⅜" casing

Attach the Side Panel Pockets to the Side Panels

1 With the wrong side of the pocket to the right side of the panel, center the bottom of the pocket to the center bottom edge of the side panel.

2 Pin the top edge of the pocket to the side panel. The elastic edge will stretch a little to reach the sides of the panel.

3 Pin the pocket edges at a 90-degree angle from the top to the bottom edge as shown.

4 Make two tucks one on either side of the center base of the pockets as shown.

5 Sew the pockets to the panel. Backstitch at both ends.

6 Sew the ⅜"-wide floral trim over the pocket side seams as shown. Set it aside. Repeat Steps 1-5 for the other pocket.

Make the 24" Zipper Panel

1 Lay the 5" x 24" decorator zipper panel face down. Spray both sides of the 5" x 24" batting rectangle with quilt basting spray; lay it on top of the decorator panel. Place the 5" x 24" checkerboard zipper panel lining face up.

2 Quilt in a loopy design, or as desired. See Getting Started for details.

3 Trim the edges straight. Cut the zipper panel in half lengthwise.

4 With right sides together, sew the 24" camel zipper to the 24" side of the panel. See Getting Started for details. Set the panel aside.

Make the Front and Back

1 Lay the 24" x 31½" floral duffel front face down. Spray both sides of the 24" x 31½" batting rectangle with quilt basting spray, and place it on top of the floral duffel front. Lay the 24" x 31½" checkerboard backing/lining piece face up on top of the batting. Repeat for the duffel back pieces.

2 Quilt the layers together in a loopy design, or as desired. See Getting Started for details.

3 Trim the edges straight. Set the pieces aside.

Make the Large Flat Side Pocket

1 Lay the 8" x 14" floral piece face down. Spray both sides of the 8" x 14" batting rectangle with quilt basting spray; lay it on top of the floral piece. Lay the 8" x 14" checkerboard backing/lining piece face up on top of the batting.

2 Quilt the layers together in a loopy design. See Getting Started for details.

3 Trim the edges straight.

Add the Zipper to the Large Flat Pocket

1 Sew one 14" rose zipper to the top edge of the 14" side of the pocket. See Getting Started for details.

2 Position the quilted pocket, centering it and placing it 2" below the top edge of the duffel bag back. Pin the pocket in place.

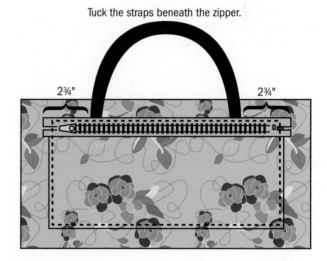

Tuck the straps beneath the zipper.

2¾"   2¾"

Cut the webbing at an angle.

3 Cut two handle straps, each 18½" long, from the 1"-wide black webbing. Fold the webbing in half; match the ends. Cut both ends at an angle as shown.

4 Tuck the handle straps beneath the zipper by ⅜"; position them 2¾" from the edges of the pocket and pin in place. Apply anti-fray solution to the ends of the webbing, and let it dry. Sew around all three sides of the pocket and across the zipper top; backstitch over the handle straps for extra strength.

5 Sew the ⅜"-wide floral trim around three sides of the pocket; begin the trim at the edge of the zipper. See above.

6 Sew the ½"-wide pink and cream checkerboard ribbon to the top of the zipper; tuck under ¼" on each end to create a clean look. Extend the checkerboard ribbon over the floral ribbon as shown above.

• • • • •
Make the Large 3-D Pocket

1 Lay the 8" x 10" floral print face down. Spray both sides of the 8" x 10" batting with quilt basting spray; lay it on top of the 8" x 10" floral print. Lay the 8" x 10" checkerboard backing/lining piece face up on top of the batting.

2 Quilt the layers together in a loopy design, or as desired. See Getting Started for details.

3 Trim the rectangle down to 7" x 9". Set the piece aside.

4 Baste the 1½" x 14½" floral strips and checkerboard lining pieces, wrong sides together, ⅛" from the edge. Repeat with the 3⅛" x 17½" floral strips and checkerboard lining pieces.

• • • • •
Add the Zipper to the Large 3-D Pocket

1 Sew one 14" rose zipper to the 14½" side of the above floral/checkerboard pieces. See Getting Started for details.

2 With right sides together, sew the strip made in Step 4 above to the zipper panel as shown. Press the seam toward the large side.

3 Topstitch across the seam next to the zipper. Sew a piece of the floral trim across the seam next to the zipper pull. Repeat Step 3 for the other side of the zipper as shown. Do not put floral trim on the opposite end unless desired.

Add the floral trim.

Sew the Large 3-D Pocket Together

1 Mark four equal parts of the zipper panel, beginning at the center of the zipper.

2 Mark the four centers on the quilted pocket front as shown.

3 Match the pins of the zipper panel, right sides together, to the pins on the quilted pocket front. Continue to pin all around the pocket as shown.

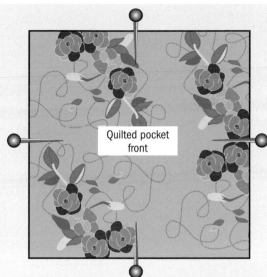

Quilted pocket front

4 As you sew around the pocket, clip the corners of the zipper panel to make them easier to turn.

5 Zigzag the seam edge and the raw edge of the pocket.

6 Press the open end of the pocket under by ¼".

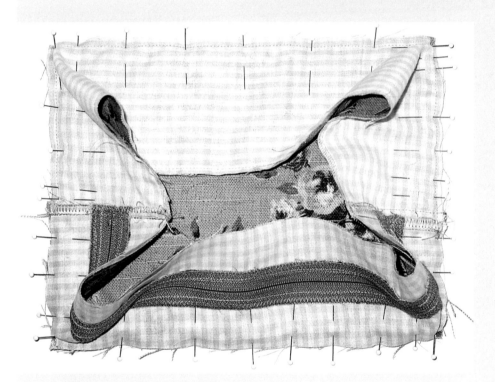

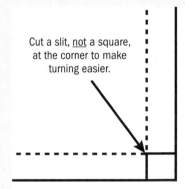

Cut a slit, <u>not</u> a square, at the corner to make turning easier.

Sew the Large 3-D Pocket to the Bag

1 Make a 6¾" x 8¾" rectangle from heavy card stock.

2 Position the card stock horizontally on the front panel so it is 1½" from the top edge and 4" from the left edge. Draw a chalk line around the card stock.

3 Pin each of the pressed-under corners of the pocket to the corners on the chalk lines.

4 Before sewing the pocket onto the bag, place the other 18" strap underneath the pocket so it is approximately 3" from the left corner of the pocket. Match the strap to the opposite side's strap.

5 Sew the pocket to the bag. Backstitch over the strap for added strength.

• • • • •
Make the Small 3-D Pocket

1 Lay the 6" x 8" floral rectangle face down. Spray both sides of the 6" x 8" batting rectangle with quilt basting spray; lay it on top of the floral rectangle. Lay the 6" x 8" checkerboard backing/lining piece face up on top of the batting.

2 Quilt the layers together in a loopy design, or as desired. See Getting Started for details. Cut the quilted piece down to 5½" x 7".

3 Baste the 1½" x 12" floral and checkerboard lining strips, wrong sides together. Repeat with the remaining floral and checkerboard strips.

4 Sew the 12" rose zipper to the strips created in Step 3. See Getting Started for details.

5 Baste the 3⅛" x 13" floral and checkerboard lining strips, wrong sides together. Sew the 12" zipper panel to the 3⅛" x 13" floral and checkerboard lining piece. Add the ⅜"-wide floral trim across the seam as done in the large 3-D pocket as shown.

6 Sew the zipper panel to the pocket front following the instructions for the Large 3-D pocket.

7 Make a 5¼" x 6¾" rectangle of card stock. Position the card stock horizontally onto the bag, next to the large pocket, and mark it with a chalk line.

8 Pin each of the corners of the pocket to the corners on the chalk lines.

9 Pin the other end of the handle underneath the small pocket approximately 3" from the right side of the pocket. Sew on the pocket, backstitching over the webbing for extra strength.

• • • • •
Make the Shoulder Strap Tabs

1 Lay one 5" square floral piece face down. Spray both sides of a 5" batting square with quilt basting spray; lay it on top of the floral square. Place a second 5" floral square face up on top of the batting. Repeat for the remaining 5" floral squares.

2 With the same color of thread in the needle and bobbin, quilt the layers as desired.

3 Use the Shoulder Strap Tab pattern to cut two shoulder strap tab pieces from the quilted squares.

4 Sew together enough bias strips to create the needed binding plus 1". Bind the shoulder strap tabs on the three shorter sides. Leave a ¼" overhang when sewing the binding on the tabs. You will need the extra length when you turn the binding to the back side. See Getting Started for details.

Add the Eyelets to the Tabs

1 Mark the eyelet holes using a pencil and the hole on the eyelet. Use sharp scissors to cut out the eyelet holes on the tabs. The fabric will stretch, so don't make the holes too big.

2 Follow the manufacturer's directions to install the eyelets. Use a hard surface, such as cement or marble, when you hammer the eyelets together. Because the eyelets are so large, you will need a harder surface to get it to stay together correctly.

Add the Piping

1 Press the packaged quilt binding open, leaving the two side folds intact. Cut the binding in half lengthwise down the center.

2 Fold the quilt binding over the packaged piping. Use a zipper foot to sew the binding on. Trim the seam down to ¼".

Fold the binding over the piping.

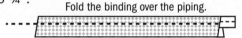

3 With raw edges together, sew the checkerboard piping on both sides of the zipper panel as shown. Zigzag the edges of the piping and zipper panel.

4 With raw edges together, sew piping around all four sides of the side panel pocket pieces. Zigzag the edges as shown.

Tip

Sewing the piping on all four sides of the side panel is different than how I originally made the duffel bag. After putting the bag together, I realized that it would be easier to sew the side panels to the duffel bag. Live and learn!

· · · · ·

Sew the Zipper Panel to the Front and Back

1 With right sides together, sew the zipper panel to the duffel bag front and back edges as shown. Zigzag the raw edges.

· · · · ·

Sew the Duffel Bag Together

1 Find the center of the side panel base and the center of the front/back bag. Mark the centers with pins.

2 Unzip the zipper so that it is easier to turn the bag right side out.

3 With right sides together, match the pins, and pin around the side panel pieces. Clip the corners for easy turning.

4 Use a zipper foot to sew around the panel; begin with the zipper panel. Start and stop at the zipper panel, backstitch at each end. Leave the bag wrong side out; it will be easier to sew together.

5 Finish sewing the rest of the side panel to the duffel bag. Backstitch at the beginning and end of the seam. Repeat with the other side.

6 Zigzag the raw edges. Turn the bag right side out.

· · · · · ·

Add the Shoulder Strap

1 Follow manufacturer's directions to add the swivel hooks and slider to the 1½"-wide webbing. See Getting Started for details.

2 Attach the shoulder hooks to the eyelets.

· · · · ·

Make the Duffel Bag Base

1 Cut an 8" x 13" piece of stiff, fusible interfacing. If needed, piece the interfacing by laying the edges close together and zigzagging over the two pieces.

2 Layer the two 8" x 13" checkerboard rectangle base pieces with right sides out, onto each side of the stiff, fusible interfacing. Iron the fabric onto each side of the fusible interfacing to cover it.

3 Zigzag around all four sides of the fabric-covered insert.

4 Place the insert in the bottom of the duffel.

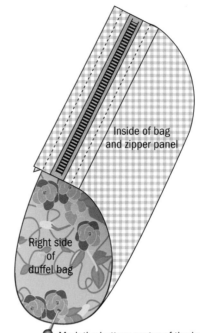

Inside of bag and zipper panel

Right side of duffel bag

Mark the bottom center of the bag with a pin.

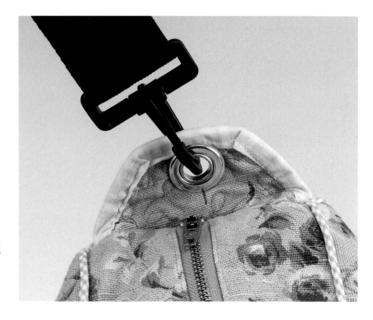

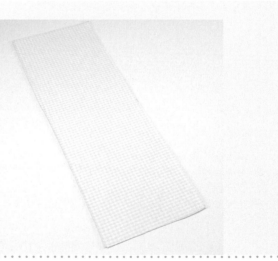

CONTRIBUTORS AND RESOURCES

Contributors

Ancient Earth Echoes Designs

Tassel fibers
HC 61 Box 60
Ramah, NM 87321
Phone: 505-290-0844
E-mail: teresa@earthechoes.biz
Web: www.earthechoes.biz

Atlas Gloves

Nitrile Touch Quilter's Glove
851 Coho Way
Bellingham, WA 98225
Web: www.lfsinc.com

Berwick Offray LLC

Satin and grosgrain ribbons
Ninth and Bomboy Lane
Berwick, PA 18603
Phone: 800-327-0350
Web: www.offray.com

Beacon Adhesives Inc.

Gem-Tac and Fabri-Tac craft adhesives
125 MacQuesten Parkway S.
Mount Vernon, NY 10550
Phone: 800-865-7238
E-mail: Crafts@BeaconAdhesives.com
Web: www.beaconcreates.com

Beadalon

Eye pins
Phone: 866-423-2325
Web: www.beadalon.com

Blumenthal Lansing Co.

Webbing, buckles, findings and buttons
Phone: 563-538-4211
Web: www.buttonsplus.com

C&T Publishing

fast2fuse double-sided stiff,
    fusible interfacing
1651 Challenge Drive
Concord, CA 94520-5206
Phone: 800-284-1114
Web: www.ctpub.com

The C-Thru Ruler Co.

¼" ruler
6 Britton Drive
Bloomfield, CT 06002
Phone: 800-243-8419
Web: www.cthruruler.com

Clover Needlecraft Inc.

Sewing and quilting notions, including
    cutting tools, magnet snaps, swivel ring,
    strap slide, hand sewing needles and glass-
    head pins
13438 Alondra Blvd.
Cerritos, CA 90703
E-mail: cni@clover-usa.com
Web: www.clover-usa.com

Coats & Clark

All-purpose thread, invisible thread, multi-
    colored thread and zippers
P.O. Box 12229
Greenville, SC 29612-0229
Phone: 800-648-1479
Web: www.coatsandclark.com

DMC Inc.

Embroidery floss
South Hackensack Avenue
Port Kearny Building 10F
South Kearny, NJ 07032
Phone: 973-589-0606
Web: www.dmc-usa.com

Expo International Inc.

Silk flower trim and furry trim
5631 Braxton Drive
Houston, TX 77036
Phone: 800-542-4367
Web: www.expointl.com

Fairfield Processing Corp.

Web: www.poly-fil.com

Fiskars Brands Inc., USA

Pliers and cutting tools
2537 Daniels St.
Madison, WI 53718
Phone: 866-348-5661
E-mail: socconsumeraffairs@fiskars.com
Web: www.fiskars.com

General Pencil Company

White chalk pencil
P.O. Box 5311
Redwood City, CA 94063
Phone: 650-369-4889
E-mail: info@generalpencil.com
Web: www.generalpencil.com/

Gingher Inc.

Shears
322-D Edwardia Drive
Greensboro, NC 27409
Phone: 800-446-4437
E-mail: info@gingher.com
Web: www.gingher.com

Hobbs Bonded Fibers

Battings, pillow inserts and fiberfill
P.O. Box 2521
Waco, TX 76702-2521
Phone: 800-433-3357
Web: www.hobbsbondedfibers.com

JHB International

Stitchin' Up the Pieces buttons
1955 South Quince St.
Denver, CO 80231
Phone: 303-751-8100
Web: www.buttons.com

June Tailor

Assorted sewing and quilting notions and
    tools, including Sew Station and Quilt
    Basting Spray
P.O. Box 208
Richfield, WI 53076
Phone: 800-844-5400
E-mail: customerservice@junetailor.com
Web: www.junetailor.com

Krause Publications

Publisher of this and other quality how-to
    books for sewing, quilting, machine em-
    broidery and other crafts.
700 E. State St.
Iola, WI 54990-0001
Phone: 888-457-2873
Web: www.krausebooks.com

Lolly Corp.

Lickity Grip
18950 U.S. Highway 441, No. 213
Mount Dora, FL 32757
Phone: 877-BY-LOLLY
Web: www.lollycorp.com

Mountain Mist

100 percent cotton Cream Rose batting
2551 Crescentville Road
Cincinnati, OH 45241
Phone: 800-345-7150
E-mail; mountainmist@legett.com
Web: www.stearnstextiles.com

Nifty-Thrifty Dry Goods

Ribbon and trims
Barrington, R.I.
Phone: 401-246-0863

Olfa

Rotary cutting tools, rulers and mats
5500 N. Pearl St., Suite 400
Rosemont, IL 60018
Phone: 800-962-OLFA
Web: www.olfa.com

P&B Textiles

Fabric
1580 Gilbreth Road
Burlingame, CA 94010
Phone: 650-692-0422
Web: www.pbtex.com

Pellon

Wonder Under lightweight fusible webbing
Phone: 770-491-8001 Ext. 2986
E-mail: CustomerService@ShopPellon.com

Prym Consumer USA

Sewing, quilting, cutting and craft-related
    tools and notions, including Fray Check,
    InnerFuse, Omnigrid and Omnigrip
    products
P.O. Box 5028
Spartanburg, SC 29304
Web: www.dritz.com

RJR Fabrics

Fabrics
2203 Dominguez St., Building K-3
Torrance, CA 90501
Phone: 800-422-5426
E-mail: info@rjrfabrics.com
Web: www.rjrfabrics.com

Rowenta

Steamers and irons
196 Boston Ave.
Medford, MA 02155
Phone: 781-396-0600
Web: www.rowenta.com

Schmetz

80/12 quilting sewing machine needles
Web: www.schmetz.com

Sulky of America

KK 2000 Temporary Spray Adhesive and
    Blendables thread
P.O. Box 494129
Port Charlotte, FL 33949-4129
Phone: 800-874-4115
E-mail: info@sulky.com
Web: www.sulky.com

The Beadery Craft Products

3-n-1 tool, Salway beads and lamp work
   beads
P.O. Box 178
Hope Valley, RI 02832
Phone: 401-539-2432
E-mail: info@thebeadery.com
Web: www.thebeadery.com/

The Warm Co.

Batting and fusible products, including
   Steam-a-Seam2
954 E. Union St.
Seattle, WA 98122
Phone: 800-234-9276
E-mail: info@warmcompany.com
Web: www.warmcompany.com

Timber Lane Press

Timtex stiff interfacing
Timber Lane, Idaho
Phone: 208-664-2664
Web: www.timtexstore.com/

Wrights

EZ Quilting tools, trims and embellishments,
   rayon cording
85 South St.
P.O. Box 398
West Warren, MA 01092
Phone: 800-660-0415
Web: www.wrights.com
Web: www.ezquilt.com

White Sewing Machines

Quilter's Star sewing machine and assorted
   presser feet
31000 Viking Parkway
Westlake, OH 44145
Phone: 800-331-3164
Web: www.whitesewing.com

Resources

Annie's Attic

Web: www.anniesattic.com

Baby Lock

Web: www.babylock.com

Bernina of America

Web: www.berninausa.com

Brother

Web: www.brother-usa.com

Clotilde LLC

Web: www.clotilde.com

Connecting Threads

Web: www.ConnectingThreads.com

Elna USA

Web: www.elnausa.com

Ghee's

Web: www.ghees.com

Herrschners Inc.

Web: www.herrschners.com

Home Sew

Web: www.homesew.com

Husqvarna Viking Sewing Machine Co.

Web: www.husqvarnaviking.com

Janome

Web: www.janome.com

Keepsake Quilting

Web: www.keepsakequilting.com

Kenmore

Web: www.sears.com

Nancy's Notions

Web: www.nancysnotions.com

Pfaff

Web: www.pfaffusa.com

Singer

Web: www.singerco.com

Tacony Corp.

Web: www.tacony.com